The Book of Wine

An Introduction to Choosing,
Serving, and Drinking the
Best Wines

Jackson Meyer

adamsmedia
Avon, Massachusetts

Published by
Adams Media, a division of F+W Media, Inc.
57 Littlefield Street, Avon, MA 02322. U.S.A.
www.adamsmedia.com

Contains material adapted and abridged from *The Everything® Wine Book, 3rd Edition* by
David White, copyright © 2014, 2010, 2005, 1997 by F+W Media, Inc., ISBN 10:
1-4405-8342-0, ISBN 13: 978-1-4405-8342-1; *The Only Wine Book You'll Ever Need* by
Danny May, copyright © 2004 by F+W Media, Inc., ISBN 10: 1-59337-101-2, ISBN
13: 978-1-59337-101-2.

ISBN 10: 1-4405-8457-5
ISBN 13: 978-1-4405-8457-2
eISBN 10: 1-4405-8458-3
eISBN 13: 978-1-4405-8458-9

Printed in the United States of America.

10 9 8 7 6 5 4 3 2 1

Library of Congress Cataloging-in-Publication Data
Meyer, Jackson, author.
  The book of wine / Jackson Meyer.
    pages cm
  Includes index.
  ISBN 978-1-4405-8457-2 (pob) -- ISBN 1-4405-8457-5 (pob) -- ISBN 978-1-
4405-8458-9 (ebook) -- ISBN 1-4405-8458-3 (ebook)
  1. Wine and wine making--History. I. Title.
  TP549.M49 2015
  641.2'2--dc23
                              2014033052

Cover design by Elisabeth Lariviere.
Cover image © Maxim Ibragimov/123RF.

This book is available at quantity discounts for bulk purchases.
For information, please call 1-800-289-0963.

Contents

Introduction

Malbec. Shiraz. Prosecco. You've enjoyed these wines at dinner parties and ordered them at restaurants. But now it's time to learn more about these, and other, vintages—and prepare to soak in everything you need to know about today's most popular wines.

The Book of Wine opens the door to the deliciously complex world of wine and gives you the information you need to choose wines for any occasion; identify the nuances of different varietals by taste, smell, and region; and order and serve wine like an expert. In addition, you'll find information on what to serve with the wine you bring home from your local winery or vintner, how to connect with vintners around the world, and how to explore wines from different regions—and different grapes—to expand your palate.

Throughout the book, you'll also find pricing information that will allow you to choose the best wine for the occasion, whether you're hosting a party for your friends or picking out a bottle to celebrate a special occasion:

- $ = $10–$25
- $$ = $25–$50
- $$$ = $50–$100
- $$$$ = $100+

Keep in mind that, in all lists of recommended wines, prices and availability may vary.

So sit back, take a sip, and let *The Book of Wine* teach you everything you need to know about wine—from grape to glass.

PART 1

Wine 101

CHAPTER 1

A Brief History of Wine

The discovery of wine was probably an accident. It didn't have to be "invented," because wine can happen all by itself. It's safe to assume that, way back, people learned to store their fruits of summer for the bleak winters ahead. More than likely, they put their grapes into a hollow in a rock, where nature took over, and fermentation turned the grapes into a bubbling liquid, which we now call wine.

Wine in the Ancient World

We may not know how humans were first introduced to wine, but we do know that people have been imbibing since at least 4000 B.C., perhaps as far back as 6000 B.C., and maybe even further back than that. Mesopotamia (Persia), near present-day Iran and Egypt—the endpoints of the Fertile Crescent—seems to be the birthplace of ancient winemaking, and recent discoveries point to winemaking in China during the same period.

A Persian fable has it that an ancient king kept his beloved grapes in an earthen jar labeled "poison." A discontented member of his harem drank juice from the jar in a suicide attempt, but instead of dying, she found her spirits quite rejuvenated. She shared the drink with her king, who took her into his favor and decreed that, henceforth, grapes would be allowed to ferment.

Ancient Persia was truly wine country. Not only did the Persians give toasts to their gods with wine, they also paid salaries in wine. Men earned ten to twenty quarts a month, and women earned ten. The grape varieties they used to make wine are believed to be the precursors of those used today.

The ancient Egyptians cultivated grapes and made wine in a surprisingly modern fashion. They developed the first arbors and pruning methods, and their grapes were stomped and fermented in large wooden vats. The wine was mostly sweet white wine, probably made from the grape now known as the Muscat of Alexandria. As a matter of respect to the gods, the Egyptians used wine in their funeral rites. Depending on the status held by the deceased, his body and belongings were anointed with wine prior to being entombed.

Situated between Egypt and Mesopotamia along the Fertile Crescent were the Phoenicians, who sailed the Mediterranean from what is now the coast of Lebanon. Thus the grapevine—and wine—found its way to Greece, Sicily, and north-central Italy.

During ancient times, everyone drank wine and beer, even children. That's not as decadent as it might sound. Frankly, drinking the water was hazardous to one's health, and wine was a good substitute thirst quencher. If you sipped one of those old-style wines today, you would probably notice that it tastes more like vinegar with a hint of cider and possesses a fairly low alcohol content. It was certainly better than the water that was available. While wine was a staple of daily life, it was consumed mostly by the rich and powerful. Beer was the drink of the common folk.

Greeks Democratize Wine

Greeks embraced wine drinking more enthusiastically than any culture before them. Wine became a drink not just for the elite, but for everyone. It is said that of all the vessels Greeks used daily, more than half related to the consumption of wine. Wine was considered to be a gift from Dionysus, the patron god and symbol of wine, and it was used in religious rituals. Greek doctors, including Hippocrates, even prescribed it for their patients.

Wine Wisdom

Retsina is a traditional wine of Greece with a long history and the distinctive taste of pine resin. The taste that permeated the wine in ancient times became so accepted that long after resin-caulked containers were discontinued, chunks of resin were added to the wine during fermentation to reproduce the flavor. Most people who have tried retsina—Greeks included—say it's an acquired taste.

Greeks considered it barbaric to drink wine straight, so they diluted it in varying proportions with water. They also learned to add herbs and spices to mask spoilage. Greeks typically stored their wine in porous clay jugs, which had to be sealed to preserve the wine. They caulked the jugs with the resin of pine trees, which imparted its unique essence.

Wine was important to the economies of Greek cities. It was traded within Greece and exported throughout the

Mediterranean world. As Greece began to colonize the western Mediterranean, the Greeks took their grapevines and winemaking technology with them.

Romans Advance Winemaking

The Roman Empire covered, at its greatest outward expansion, most of the Mediterranean lands and a good part of Europe. The Romans found grapes already under cultivation in many of their conquered lands, the wine culture having been widely distributed by their Greek and Phoenician predecessors. The Romans, too, loved wine and fostered its development throughout the empire.

By about 1000 B.C., Romans were classifying grape varieties, charting ripening characteristics, identifying diseases, and increasing yields through irrigation and fertilization. They developed wooden barrels to store the wines in place of the skins and jars previously used. The Romans may have been the first to put wine into glass containers.

By the first century A.D., Rome was awash with wine. Each person in the city of Rome drank on average half a liter each day. Winemaking techniques had spread from Italy to Spain, Germany, England, and France, and those regions developed their own vineyards. You could certainly call this the world's first wine boom. Corner bars popped up all over cities such as Pompeii. The supply (or oversupply) of wine drove down the prices, so much so that Emperor Domitian ordered the great vineyards of France be uprooted to eliminate the competition of French wines with the local Italian wines. Fortunately, that order wasn't fully executed, and it was rescinded two centuries later.

Wine in Europe

Wine has always been associated with spirituality and religion. While most of the religions practiced in the eastern Mediterranean incorporated wine in their rituals, it was the spread of Christianity in the fourth century that ensured the survival of viticulture and winemaking after the collapse of the Roman Empire. Because wine was such an integral part in the celebration of the Eucharist, the monasteries and cathedrals that sprang up across Europe took up winemaking and amassed substantial vineyard holdings. The monks—who had the education, the financial resources of the Catholic Church, and the requisite time for cultivating land and trying new techniques—became some of the most important winemakers of the Middle Ages.

Monastic wineries established extensive vineyards across Europe—and especially in Burgundy, Bordeaux, Champagne, the Loire Valley, and the Rhône Valley. During this time, France emerged as the preeminent winemaking region in the world.

Wine and War Don't Mix

In 1152, Henry II of England married France's Eleanor of Aquitaine, whose dowry included the vineyard areas of Bordeaux and neighboring Gascony. The light red wine produced there gained favor in England and came to be called claret. By 1350, the port city of Bordeaux was shipping a million cases of claret a year, but the sporadic fighting between the kings of England and France—known as the Hundred Years' War (1337–1453)—put an end to England's access to her much-loved wine. Any ship transporting the wine faced piracy, and protecting the ships became prohibitively expensive. England had to look beyond western France for wine imports.

A trading friendship with Portugal began that ultimately led to the creation of port wine. The journey by sea from Portugal to England was hard on wine. The shippers in Oporto, the port city, began adding buckets of brandy to the wine to stabilize it so it would arrive in good condition. They started adding the brandy earlier and earlier until they were adding it during fermentation. This wine became known as, quite appropriately, porto—or port.

Reaching Out to the New World

With the discovery and colonization of new lands, emigrating Europeans took their vines and their winemaking knowledge elsewhere. Exploration and settlement brought wine to the Americas and South Africa in the 1500s and 1600s and to Australia in the 1700s. The wine history of Europe thus became intertwined—for better and for worse—with that of the New World.

Wine in the Americas

The wine-guzzling conquistadors who arrived in South and Central America from Spain in the 1500s were responsible—directly or indirectly—for introducing winemaking to those lands. Hernando Cortés, perhaps the most successful of the conquistadors and later governor of Mexico, defeated the Aztecs in 1521. After much celebration, he and his soldiers were out of wine. One of his first orders of business was to direct all new Spanish settlers to plant vines on the land they'd been granted. Winemaking flourished. In fact, it flourished to such an extent that the settlers needed to import less and less wine from Spain.

The king of Spain, who wanted a captive market for Spanish goods, wasn't happy about this. He levied heavy taxes and ordered vineyards destroyed in all of Spain's new colonies. The edict was enforced most aggressively in Mexico, and the growth of the burgeoning wine industry there came to an abrupt halt.

The church was the sole exception to the king's edict. Just like in Europe, vineyards survived under the care of the church. Missions—particularly Jesuit missions—were established early in Chile, Argentina, Peru, and Mexico. Later, a series of missions along the Pacific Coast would bring winemaking to California.

Wine Wisdom

Mexico is home to the oldest commercial winery in the Americas. The first wine was produced there in 1596. The winery was known as "Santa Maria de las Parras"—or Holy Mary of the Vines. It still operates today as Casa Madero in the Parras Valley.

Colonial Experiments in North America

Early settlers brought with them a mighty thirst for wine. Imagine their delight when they found a landscape practically smothered by grapevines. Upon closer inspection, however, they found vines unlike any they were familiar with back in Europe. Being the pioneers they were, they forged ahead and fermented anyway. The first wine from native American grapes was made in Jamestown in 1609, and it paled to what they had consumed in Europe.

The colonists' next step was to import vine cuttings of *Vitis vinifera* from Europe so they could grow familiar varieties such as Cabernet Sauvignon, Merlot, and Chardonnay. All up and down the Atlantic coast settlers planted vines from every great European wine region. Even Thomas Jefferson planted vines at Monticello. No one succeeded. Each vineyard would die off after only two or three years. It was thought that the extremes of weather were the reason for failure, or that indigenous diseases were at fault.

Even though the *vinifera* vines failed, the side effect of these experiments was the emergence in the 1800s of new American hybrid varieties. These hybrids became the foundation for the wine industry in the eastern United States. Winemaking centers emerged in Ohio, Missouri, on the shores of Lake Erie, and in the Finger Lakes region of upstate New York. The American wine industry was on its way.

California Dreamin'

Beginning around 1770, Franciscan monks established missions—and planted vineyards—up the coast of what would become California. Father Junípero Serra led the way when he planted the first vineyard at Mission San Diego. He traveled north and established eight more missions. His work gave him the name "the father of California wine."

The gold rush of 1849 brought frenzied growth, both in terms of population and vineyards. By this time Sonoma had 22,000 acres under vine, and Napa had 18,000. The Santa Clara Valley and Livermore Valley were widely planted and had numerous wineries at this same time. Many pioneer vintners settled south and east of the San Francisco Bay where most of the bottling plants were located. Railroads arrived, and now California wines were available in eastern markets and shipped around the world. By the end of the century, all of the state's winemaking regions were producing wine. California had become the premier wine-growing region in the country.

Prohibition Wipes Out an Industry

The winemaking business has had its ups and downs, sometimes due to insects and other times to economics. In 1920, however, it crashed and burned because of politics. The Eighteenth Amendment to the U.S. Constitution prohibited the production, transport, and sale of alcohol.

"Prohibition" did not spring up from nowhere. In 1816, Indiana forbade Sunday sales of alcohol. In the 1840s, "dry" towns and counties emerged in seven states. In 1851, Maine outlawed the manufacture and sale of alcohol. By 1855, New Hampshire, Vermont, Delaware, Michigan, Indiana, Iowa, Minnesota, Nebraska, Connecticut, Rhode Island, Massachusetts, and New York had followed suit. At the outbreak of World War I, thirty-three states were dry.

The Eighteenth Amendment was ratified on January 29, 1919, and one year later Prohibition began, making virtually all alcoholic beverages illegal. Even after ratification by the states, the amendment still needed an act of Congress to make it enforceable. That came in the form of the Volstead Act, spearheaded by the Minnesota congressman of the same name. Many supporters of the Eighteenth Amendment had assumed that the "intoxicating liquors" to be banned were the high-alcohol distilled spirits, with 40 percent alcohol. Sadly, Volstead defined intoxicating liquors as any beverage containing more than 0.5 percent alcohol, thus including beer, with its 3–7 percent alcohol, and wine, with its less than 13 percent alcohol.

Lasting Effects

The almost immediate result of these acts was the decimation of the American wine industry. Vineyards were uprooted. Equipment was abandoned. Growers and producers—if they didn't go completely under—had to find creative ways to stay in business. Cooking wine could still be produced, as long as it was salted and undrinkable. Sacramental and religious wines were still allowed, as well as wine made for medicinal purposes. Home producers were permitted to make up to 200 gallons of wine a year.

Prohibition's damage to the wine industry was far more than economic; it was cultural. The art of winemaking, which had been practiced for centuries, became illegal. People who had invested their lives and savings in research and equipment had their investments wiped out. Thousands of workers involved in making, bottling, distributing, serving, and selling wine were out of jobs. In 1919, the United States produced 55 million gallons of wine. In 1925, the nation produced just 3.5 million gallons.

By 1933, when the Twenty-first Amendment repealed Prohibition, the damage had been done. The country had lost its winemakers and an entire generation of wine drinkers. Other effects of this "Noble Experiment" exist to this day in the form of direct-shipping and distribution laws. By 1936, fifteen states had laws that created state monopolies on wine sales and prevented free-market competition. Other states, while allowing hotels and restaurants to serve wine, banned bars and "liquor by the drink." The aftermath of Prohibition resulted in a hodgepodge of alcohol laws that vary from state to state and community to community.

The Wine Boom in the United States

When Prohibition was repealed, the wine industry was slow to recover. In the early days following the repeal, the quality of wine was poor, in part because California grape growers were raising grapes that shipped well, rather than grapes that made fine wine. Wineries mostly sold their wines to wholesalers who bottled them under their own brands and then, in turn, sold them under generic names like Chablis and Burgundy. In 1940, Americans were drinking one gallon of wine a year per person. The average French resident, by comparison, was consuming forty gallons annually. Nevertheless, the American wine industry did recover.

A major development that helped this process was the introduction of French hybrids. French hybrids crossed American and European vines to resist *phylloxera*. They were hardy enough to withstand a northeastern winter, yet yielded good-quality wine without the "grapey" taste of native varieties.

JFK and Julia Child Join Forces

The American wine boom really began with the affluence of the late 1950s. Wine was attractive to educated suburbanites, especially those wealthy enough to travel abroad. Wine, which to most of the wine-drinking world is a simple beverage, had become a status symbol in the United States.

A few role models helped. When John F. Kennedy was sworn in he brought with him, among other things, a new sense of internationalism. His wife, Jackie, adored all things French. French restaurants—and French wines—became very trendy, and from a kitchen in a Boston television studio, Julia Child taught a generation of Americans how to prepare French cuisine and how to match it with French wine.

New products appeared in wine stores to meet the growing demand. Portuguese rosé in the form of Mateus and Lancers hit the shelves. They were sweet and slightly fizzy, but fruity. Their Europe provenance gave them cachet. West

Germany contributed Liebfraumilch, a flowery, fruity, and slightly sweet blend of Riesling and other grape varieties.

Meanwhile, California's reputation for world-class fine wines grew rapidly. In the early 1970s, resourceful wine-makers, many educated in their craft at the University of California at Davis, finally established California as a world-class wine region. In a blind tasting that pitted several California wines against top French wines in 1976, the American wines—Stag's Leap Wine Cellars Cabernet Sauvignon and Chateau Montelena Chardonnay—won. The decision, by a panel of all French judges, shocked the world.

Varietals Take Over

American winemakers soon began the practice of labeling their wines according to the grape varieties used to make them. This was in direct contrast to the European custom of labeling wines according to place of origin. Ordering a glass of "white wine" was replaced with ordering a glass of "Chardonnay."

Americans became attached to their new varietals. One California variety, however, wasn't having as much success in the 1970s: Zinfandel.

Many growers had acre upon acre of Zinfandel vines, whose grapes matured effortlessly in the California sunshine. But demand for white wine outpaced supply, so many wine-makers started producing white wine from red grapes, taking advantage of the fact that even red grapes give off white juice. Many even contemplated replanting their vineyards with other varieties.

In 1975, the winemaker at Sutter Home, Bob Trinchero, had a problem while making his White Zinfandel. A portion of the wine experienced a "stuck fermentation," meaning the yeast died before all the sugar had converted into alcohol.

Rather than "fix" the fruity, pink, slightly sweet rosé by adding more yeast, Trinchero decided to let it sit for two weeks. When he revisited the wine, he knew it would be a hit. He was right—it was an instant and enormous success in the American market. Its popularity helped to drive yearly wine consumption in the United States up to two gallons per person.

The Last Twenty Years

Americans' taste in wines continues to change. The proliferation of wine classes, tastings, dinners, and publications has certainly been beneficial. While White Zinfandel is still a staple for millions, there's an enthusiasm for venturing beyond those pink borders. The White Zin craze morphed into a Chardonnay trend, a Merlot fad, and the embrace of Pinot Grigio, Pinot Noir, Shiraz, and Malbec. There will always be new wines in vogue.

In recent years, international collaboration and international competition have picked up. Famous names in wine—Mondavi, Lafite Rothschild, Lapostolle—have invested heavily in land and facilities in places like South America to produce high-quality wines. There has been consolidation, too, with larger wine companies buying up smaller brands. This consolidation has enabled one producer to market many brands and gain shelf space in retail stores. For consumers, the positive effect of consolidation is lower prices and ease of purchase; the downside is reduced exposure to smaller but equally good producers. This should not be a serious cause of alarm, however, because as the number of educated wine drinkers grows, the demand for choice in the wine market will doubtless make the wines of boutique producers more accessible. Indeed, more producers from more regions than ever before are vying for space in the wine market.

CHAPTER 2

Types of Wine

Wine labels usually—but not always—tell us what we need to know about the wine we are buying. Certain terms are obvious and self-explanatory, while others may seem obscure or misleading. Here is an explanation of some label terms you are likely to see.

Table Wine

The term "table wine" has several different meanings. On European labels it may suggest common, everyday wine of little distinction, not good enough for any of the "quality wine" designations. In some regions—particularly in Tuscany—it might indicate that a wine, though perfectly good, does not conform to traditional, local winemaking practices and, thus, is ineligible to display the name of its birthplace. As used on wine labels in the United States, "table wine" is by federal law grape wine, either sweet or dry, and not in excess of 14 percent alcohol. Some Californian producers use the term "table wine" when they don't use enough of any one grape variety (75 percent) for "varietal" labeling. For our purposes in this book we consider "table wine" to be still (not sparkling) wine with alcohol below 16 percent and dry (with no perceptible sugar) or only slightly sweet—in other words, wine that you would typically have with dinner. This would include dry white wine, dry red wine, dry rosé wine, and slightly sweet rosé wine.

White Table Wine

White table wine isn't really white. White table wine is made from green-, yellow-, or even dark-skinned grapes that are pressed in such a way that the light-colored juice runs freely from the grapes without drawing much color or extract from the skins. The naturally occurring sugar in the juice then ferments to between 8 percent and 15 percent alcohol, leaving almost no residual sugar behind. "Chardonnay" is a white table wine, one that is labeled by the primary grape variety used in its production. "Sancerre" is another white table wine, labeled by its geographic origin. To be labeled as "Sancerre" the wine must conform to French government standards dictating the grape variety (Sauvignon Blanc in this case), crop yield per acre, and other factors.

(For lists of specific white table wine recommendations, see Chapter 4.)

Red Table Wine

Red table wine ranges in hue from light brick red to deep purple to almost black. The color comes from the skins. Unlike white grapes, the grapes for red wine production are crushed, and the juice and the skins get a prolonged soaking (up to a month) before the mash of crushed grapes (the "must") is gently pressed to separate the juice. While some red grapes, especially those grown in the hotter parts of California, may develop very high sugar levels, red wine, like white wine, rarely ferments to levels higher than 15 percent on its own. Like white table wines, red table wines may be labeled by grape variety, geographic origin, or by a brand name.

(For lists of specific red table wine recommendations, see Chapter 4.)

Rosé Wine

There are great white wines and there are great red wines. However, we never hear anyone call a rosé wine great. Perhaps that is because rosé wine has characteristics of both red and white wine, but not the best characteristics; kind of like cross-breeding a supermodel and a physicist, only to produce offspring with the scientist's looks and the model's brains.

Rosé table wine can be made several different ways: Red wine grapes (such as Zinfandel) may be vinified as if they were white wine grapes, with just enough skin contact to impart a "blush" of pinkness; or, more simply, unfinished red and white wine may be blended in such proportions as to yield a light, pink-colored wine. Rosé table wines are often bottled with a hint or more of sweetness, perhaps because they might otherwise be charmless. However, the bone-dry rosé table wines of France and Spain are considered to be the best in the world, if only enjoyable during the hot summer months, when food and wine are less formal.

Rosés of the World

Name	Region	Price
Château de Montgueret "Rosé de Loire"	Loire Valley, France	$
Viña Sardosol	Navarra, Spain	$
Bonny Doon, "Vin Gris de Cigare" Pink Wine	California	$
Canto Perdrix, Tavel	Rhône, France	$
Château d'Aqueria, Tavel	Rhône, France	$

Note: In all lists of recommended wines, prices and availability may vary.

Sparkling Wine, or Bubbly

"Come, for I am drinking stars!" So said Benedictine cellar master Dom Pérignon, according to legend, when he tasted the first "champagne." (In reality, the bubbles in champagne came long after the monk's death.)

A generation ago, a dutiful husband knew enough to pick up a bottle of champagne on his way home from work for special occasions such as his wife's birthday, their anniversary, St. Valentine's Day, and New Year's Eve. These may well have been the only four times that a couple drank wine of any sort. Today, however, the American public is far savvier when it comes to choosing wine, and the wine dollars that once went toward champagne might now be spent on very good Chardonnay or Merlot. Wine is a regular part of many people's lifestyles these days.

However, champagne has become a victim of the wine boom, in large part because it has never lost its association with celebrations and special events. That is a pity. Quality champagnes and other sparkling wines are simply good wines with bubbles, and they are generally excellent food wines. Despite the common perception, they need not be any more expensive than anything else you would drink.

The Origins of Champagne

Champagne derives its name from the district in Northern France where it is produced—a region in which wine has been made since Roman times. It was not until the early 1800s that "champagne" became synonymous with effervescent white (or pink) wine.

The bubbles in champagne are the result of a second fermentation that takes place within the sealed bottle. When yeast cells transform sugar into ethyl alcohol, they produce carbon dioxide gas as well. Over several centuries, champagne producers perfected the technique of putting still (nonsparkling) wine in sturdy bottles, adding yeast and sugar, and sealing the bottle with a temporary stopper to keep the carbon dioxide from escaping. In order to produce a crystal-clear sparkling wine, the remaining dead yeast cells must be quickly removed so as not to lose the effervescence. This technique is known as the "Champagne method" and often appears on wine labels as "*méthode champenoise*."

Grape Varieties in Sparkling Wines

French champagne is made from three different grape varieties: the dark-skinned Pinot Noir and Pinot Meunier, which barely ripen so far north; and Chardonnay. Bottles labeled "Blanc de Noirs" are made solely from the Pinots, while "Blanc de Blancs" is made entirely from Chardonnay. Sparkling wine producers around the world tend to use Pinot Noir and/or Chardonnay, while Pinot Meunier is rarely cultivated outside of the Champagne district.

Other Types of Sparkling Wines

The French prefer to keep the name "champagne" for wines produced in their Champagne district by this painstaking method. However, sparkling wine is produced throughout the world, under a variety of names, including:

- **Cava** from Spain
- **Sekt** from Germany
- **Prosecco** from the Veneto region of Italy
- **Sparkling Shiraz**, a highly unusual but delicious version produced in Australia

Much to the annoyance of the French, it is allowable under United States law to label sparkling wine as "champagne" (with a small "c") as long as the label indicates the geographic origin (such as "California" or "New York State") and the method by which the wine got its sparkle. Aside from the labor-intensive (and expensive) *méthode champenoise*, there are other, less expensive ways to produce bubbles, such as the "charmat bulk process" or the "transfer method." These terms—or their euphemisms—will appear on the wine label.

Champagne and sparkling wine labels will often (but not always) give an indication of the beverage's degree of sweetness. In the Champagne method, sugar is often added to the bottle after the dead yeast is removed in order to balance the flavor. Following is a quick listing of common label terms that indicate champagne's level of sweetness:

- **Brut** indicates an added sugar content of 15 grams per liter (about a tablespoon per bottle) or less.
- **Extra Dry** is slightly sweeter.

- **Demi-sec** is sweet enough for dessert.
- **Brut Nature or Brut Sauvage** indicates that no sugar has been added.

Champagne and Sparkling Wine from Around the World

Name	Region	Price
Segura Viudas "Aria Brut" Cava	Catalonia, Spain	$
Gruet Blanc de Noirs NV	New Mexico	$
Veuve Clicquot NV "Yellow Label"	Champagne, France	$$
Roederer Estate "Brut L'Ermitage"	Anderson Valley, CA	$$
Bollinger "Special Cuvée" Brut	Champagne, France	$$
Schramsberg Reserve Cuvée	California	$$$
Laurent-Perrier "Cuvée Rosé Brut" NV	Champagne, France	$$$
Moët et Chandon, Cuvée Dom Pérignon	Champagne, France	$$$$
Krug "Grande Cuvée" NV	Champagne, France	$$$$

Dessert Wine

Dessert wine, in its finest forms, displays all of the charms one expects of a great wine—intriguing aromas, layers of complex flavors, velvety texture, and a long, memorable finish. On top of all that, dessert wine is sweet enough to satisfy your inner trick-or-treater. Dessert wine truly embodies the best of everything wine has to offer in one glass. A great dessert wine has enough complexity to seduce the most jaded veteran wine lover's palate, yet it also captivates the neophyte with its luscious sweetness. While sweetness is the common denominator, there are enough different types and styles of dessert wine to constitute a parallel wine universe.

What Makes Wine Sweet?

Sweet wine is certainly not a recent development. Prior to the advent of tightly sealed bottles, wine made from raisined grapes was prized by the ancients for its sweetness as well as for its longevity, and it is likely that the earliest wines were often sweet as a result of incomplete fermentations. Modern dessert wines, sweet by design, are characterized by very high sugar levels perfectly balanced with piercing acidity. These wines come by their sweetness via several different paths, nearly always beginning with naturally occurring glucose and fructose. Concentrations of these grape sugars increase in proportion to ripeness, and fully ripe grapes usually have a sugar content sufficient to ferment into 12 percent alcohol by volume. The unfermented (residual) sugar in sweet dessert wines is the result of one of several factors—raisining, extreme ripeness, a freeze late in the harvest, fermentation-stopping fortification with brandy . . . or an infection of the mold *botrytis cinerea*, also known as "noble rot."

Just as the first wine in history was most likely the result of grapes inadvertently allowed to ferment, the first dessert wine as we know it was probably the result of a happy accident of nature. Just imagine an exasperated *vigneron* discovering a few rows of grotesquely moldy grapes and then bravely vinifying them, only to find that he has produced a delicious, sweet nectar.

Great European Dessert Wines

The vineyards of the Sauternes district in the Bordeaux region are particularly susceptible to the *botrytis* mold, which draws water from the grape while leaving the sugars alone. Because much of the water has been stolen from the affected grapes, it takes many times more grapes to yield a given quantity of wine, which commands a correspondingly steep price. The great Château d'Yquem of Sauternes is generally regarded as the world's standard-bearing dessert wine and fetches about $140 per half bottle upon release.

There are many excellent Sauternes available for a fraction of d'Yquem's price, and *botrytis*-influenced dessert wines are produced elsewhere in France and in other countries. Lesser-known *botrytized* French dessert wines include Quarts de Chaume from the Loire Valley and Sélection de Grains Nobles (SGN) wines from Alsace. Meanwhile, on the other side of the Vosges Mountains from Alsace, German jawbreakers such as "Beerenauslese" and "Trockenbeerenauslese" appear on wine labels to indicate the influence of the noble rot in Germany's sweetest Rieslings and other wines.

Frozen Grapes

In addition to the wines mentioned, Germany is perhaps best known as the original source of "eiswein," dessert wine made from grapes that have frozen on the vine. Frozen grapes leave much of their water behind as ice crystals, and thus yield wine with an unctuous and heavenly concentration of fruity sweetness. Unlike Sauternes, which can often display a deliciously muddled array of rich flavors, eiswein's flavors are typically as clear as a January night sky. It's almost as if the requisite freezing of the grapes—to 18°F for an extended period—somehow purifies the soul of the wine.

It is only natural, then, that innovative winemakers would find a less labor-intensive alternative to handpicking frozen grapes under a bone-chilling Arctic cold front. Winemaker Randall Grahm of Bonny Doon Vineyard in California was the first to short-circuit the natural grape freeze process successfully, simply by putting Muscat grapes in the freezer for a spell and then vinifying the frozen results. Instead of co-opting the term "eiswein" (or even "ice wine"), he playfully named the sweet results "Muscat Vin de Glaciere," that is, "Wine of the Icebox." Other wineries have been quicker to borrow the increasingly marketable "eiswein" or "ice wine" terms for wines produced by artificial freezing. However, the U.S. government recently formalized its long-standing objection to such terminology for American wines. Consequently, the terminology's use on wine labels is now prohibited unless the grapes actually freeze while still on the vine. The United States is not the only other country to venture into "ice wine" territory. The Canadian wine industry benefits from reliably frigid weather in late autumn and has become world famous for its consistent production of excellent—and genuine—ice wine.

Wine Wisdom

The vast majority of dessert wines are offered in half-bottles (375ml), which is the best way to buy them. A little sweetness goes a long way: A half-bottle provides enough dessert wine for four or even six people. Sugar can act as a natural wine preservative, so an unfinished bottle of dessert wine will keep in the fridge a little longer than will a partially empty bottle of dry wine. The high alcohol content of the stronger fortified wines allows them to keep for many weeks after opening.

Other Sweet Wines from Around the World

Never to be outdone by the French, Germans, or anyone else, Italian winemakers, from the Alps down to Sicily, offer their own assortment of sweet wines. There are sweet versions of Amarone, a heavy red made from dried grapes, and late-harvest versions of Soave, both from the Veneto region. Tuscany offers Vin Santo, an amber-colored wine made from dried grapes. And from Piedmont come low-alcohol sweet sparklers, both red (Brachetto d'Acqui) and white (Moscato d'Asti).

Elsewhere in the world, Tokaji Aszú, "the poor man's d'Yquem," is one of the world's great dessert wines and has been produced in Hungary since the 1600s by blending a base wine with *aszú* paste, a mash of *botrytis*-affected grapes, in varying proportions. Less famous dessert wines of one type or another are presently produced in nearly every wine-producing region in the world, but only one is sweetened by the actual addition of sugar.

Dessert Champagne

The art of champagne making, the *méthode champenoise*, has been slowly perfected over the last three centuries. After completion of the second fermentation and a lengthy repose on the dead yeast cells, the champagne bottle is "disgorged," that is, the temporary stopper is removed from the bottle and the dead yeast is quickly removed. At this crucial stage of production, the sweetness of the final bottling is determined by the *dosage*, the addition of a mixture of wine and sugar syrup. Champagne labeled as "brut" has less than 15 grams per liter of added sugar and tastes quite dry, while dessert champagne labeled as "demi-sec" has between 33 and 50 grams per liter and is noticeably sweet.

These dessert champagnes constitute only a tiny fraction of overall champagne production. Dessert wine production among *méthode champenoise* producers outside of the Champagne district is even rarer, the most notable example being

Schramsberg Crémant Demi-Sec, an ambrosially sweet sparkler made from the Flor grape, a cross of Gewürztraminer and Sémillon, in Napa Valley.

Dessert Wine from Ten Different Countries		
Name	**Region**	**Price**
Saracco, Moscato d'Asti	Piedmont, Italy	$
Gran Barquero Pedro Ximénez (750ml)	Montilla-Moriles, Spain	$
Campbells Muscat (375ml)	Rutherglen, Australia	$
Hermann J. Wiemer "Select" Ice Wine (375ml)	Finger Lakes, NY	$$
Kracher, Cuvée Beerenauslese (375ml)	Niederösterreich, Austria	$$
Klein Constantia, "Vin de Constance" (500ml)	South Africa	$$
Inniskillin, Vidal Icewine (375ml)	Niagra, Canada	$$
Château Raymond-Lafon Sauternes (375ml)	Bordeaux, France	$$
Royal Tokaji Wine Company, Essencia 1995 (500ml)	Hungary	$$$$
Keller Trockenbeerenauslese (375ml)	Rheinhessen, Germany	$$$$

Fortified Wine

Fortified wines came into being following the discovery and refinement of the distillation process, the partial vaporization of a fermented liquid in order to separate and thus concentrate its alcohol. When produced from wine, the result is known as brandy, and it was discovered that, when added to a fermenting vat in sufficient concentration (to about 18 to 20 percent alcohol), brandy stops the yeasts in their tracks, resulting in a wine with noticeable sweetness from the residual, unfermented sugar that is stronger in alcohol than typical table wine. (Hence the term "fortified.")

These fortified wines, it was found, are relatively immune to the normally damaging jostle and heat on the high seas, and thus they shipped easily and found favor in far away England. The best-known of the fortified wines are:

- **Port** (from Portugal)
- **Sherry** (from Spain)
- **Marsala** (from Sicily)
- **Madeira** (from the island of the same name)

The French, meanwhile, have some lesser-known fortified wines of their own—vin doux naturel, or "naturally sweet wine." The best known of these—the orange-hued Muscat Beaumes-de-Venise and the deep red, Grenache-based Banyuls—are both fortified with spirits to about 15 percent alcohol.

Not all fortified wine is sweet, however. Fortified wines are recognized just as much for their role in cooking recipes as they are for their drinkability. In general, the dry versions of fortified wine are superior for cooking, and are often served as apéritifs, while the sweet versions are key members of the family of dessert wines.

Port

Port, or Porto, comes from Portugal. The name, however, comes not from the country but from the city of Oporto, at the mouth of the Douro River. As the only red fortified wine, it has natural appeal among red-wine lovers who prize Port's capacity to improve with age in the bottle for many decades.

Port is sold in several different styles—Vintage, Tawny, and Ruby are the principal versions. Vintage Port, the most expensive of these, is also the easiest to produce—as long as nature cooperates; Tawny Port, so named for its brownish cast, is the result of long barrel-aging; and Ruby Port, named for its bright, unoxidized color, is an inexpensive style that is perfect for neophytes and fine cooking.

Port is made from several different red varieties that grow to extreme ripeness in Portugal's hot Douro Valley. The fruity Souzão grape, the dark-colored "Tintas"—Tinta Cão and Tinta Francisca—and the Cabernet Franc-like Touriga are blended along with other varieties in various proportions. A white Port is also produced, although it is not nearly as prized as the red versions. All (red) Port, then, starts out as "musts" from these varieties, which are allowed to ferment halfway to dryness before the addition of brandy. Since half of the natural sugar remains unfermented, the resulting fortified wine is sweet. It then begins its life in "Port pipes" (138-gallon storage casks).

Vintage Port

After two years in storage, a vintage may be "declared" by agreement of a majority of the Port producers. This means that the Port from that particular vintage is deemed to be of sufficient quality to justify offering it as top-of-the-line Vintage Port. Vintage Port is then bottled and is best aged for at least a decade. Because Vintage Port ages in the bottle, often for several decades, it deposits a substantial amount of sediment in the bottle.

Vintage Port has always been quite popular among the British, and when paired with a wedge of Stilton, the deluxe cheese of England, you have a match made in heaven. The pungent saltiness of the cheese complements the sweet richness of Vintage Port beautifully.

The Book of Wine

Tawny Port

Unlike Vintage Port, which is transferred to bottles in its youth, Tawny Port may remain in the cask for ten, twenty, or even thirty years. "Tawny" refers to the pale brown hue of these fortified wines after so long in the cask, where oxidation occurs more readily than in the bottle. With the high alcohol guarding against the formation of vinegar, the oxidation in this case improves the flavor over time. The fruit flavors of youth evolve into mellower, more subtle flavors, and the Port becomes seemingly less sweet.

Tawny Port requires far more blending skills than does vintage Port. Unless labeled "Port of the Vintage" (another form of Tawny Port), most Tawnies are blends of ports from several different years chosen for their complementary characteristics.

Ruby Port

Ruby Port, named for its bright crimson color, is a blend of young, lesser lots of Port. Again, the blender's art is of importance. Lesser lots (casks) of Port may be skillfully blended to produce an inexpensive and delicious Ruby Port.

The forthright flavors of the Ruby variety make it a perfect choice for recipes that call for this Port. The flavors of Ruby Port will endure the cooking process far better than will the other types. Also, Ruby Port is a perfect introduction to Port as you begin to explore fortified wines.

RECOMMENDED PORT PRODUCERS

Croft	Graham
Cockburn	Taylor Fladgate
Dow	Warre
Fonseca	

Sherry

Like the other types of fortified wine, Sherry owes its popularity to the British. In fact, the name "Sherry" is an Anglicization of "Jerez," the port city on the coast of Spain from which Sherry is shipped.

Sherry is made by fortifying dry white wine made from the Palomino grape grown in Southern Spain. Among wine lovers, Sherry is not as well respected as Port, perhaps because Sherry is generally less "wine-like" and complex than Port. As a result, quality Sherry is often overlooked and underpriced. And yet, quality Sherry can be an ideal substitute for a variety of hard liquor drinks.

Whereas Port, particularly vintage Port, is perceived as closely akin to fine wine by consumers, quality Sherry is regarded as a manufactured product by many people, more like liquor than wine. Indeed, the aging, fortification, and blending processes for Sherry are far more involved than those for Vintage Port.

How Sherry Is Made

All Sherry begins its life in the warm, dry vineyards of Southern Spain. Here, the Palomino grape, a variety of little use aside from Sherry production, is made into dry, still wine. This wine, called mosto, is initially fortified with brandy to an alcohol level of 15 percent and permitted to age in the presence of air. While contact with air would destroy most wines at this stage, the partially fortified mosto thrives on it. In most (but not all) of these huge barrels, a cushion of spongy yeast, called flor, develops on the surface of the wine.

In barrels with ample flor development, the wine beneath the layer of yeast is protected from oxidation and remains pale in color. The flor yeast also imparts flavor on the wine and further concentrates the alcoholic content. Sherry from these barrels is generally called "fino" and may become one of the three paler types of Sherry—Fino itself, Manzanilla, or Amontillado.

The barrels that develop little or no flor yeast yield "oloroso" Sherry, which is finished as one of the darker styles—dry Oloroso itself, sweet Amoroso, or very sweet cream Sherry. An especially rare type of Sherry is Palo Cortado, an Oloroso that develops flor yeast late in its life and can combine the finest qualities of both Finos and Olorosos.

Because the alcohol in Fino Sherries is concentrated by the flor yeast, these types of Sherries are given additional fortification only as required by importers worldwide. In Spain, Fino Sherry is often not additionally fortified and can be found at 16 percent alcohol. As such, this type of Sherry will not survive indefinitely in an opened bottle.

In contrast, the darker Oloroso Sherries usually receive a second fortification that raises the alcoholic strength to 18 to 20 percent. Because of this, Olorosos can live for a long time in the bottle after it is opened.

The blending process used in Sherry production, called the "solera" process, is unique. Barrels of young Sherry are connected to older barrels in such a manner that Sherries from different years are blended; this is why there are no vintage Sherries. You may, however, find an expensive Sherry with a year on the label. This is usually the vintage year of the oldest Sherry in the solera blend, and it might even be more than 100 years old.

Types of Sherries

There are several different types of Sherries, which range in color from light to dark, and in flavor from dry to sweet. These include:

- **Amontillado:** This Sherry was made famous by Edgar Allan Poe's short story "The Cask of Amontillado." It is most notable for its nut-like flavor and aroma. These characteristics, along with a light brown color, can develop when a fino-type Sherry ages. Like the other fino types, Amontillado is a before-dinner drink, though better served at room temperature. While the paler fino types are most enjoyable in the hot summer, Amontillado is something of an autumn apéritif with its darker, richer flavors.
- **Amoroso:** Dry Oloroso Sherry is sometimes sweetened by the addition of sweet, concentrated wine made for this purpose from Muscatel or Pedro Ximénez grapes. The result is Amoroso Sherry, a sweet after-dinner drink. Similarly, Amoroso can be darkened with the addition of specially prepared "coloring wine." Brown Sherry is an especially dark version of Amoroso Sherry.
- **Cream:** The sweetest of Sherries, if not the darkest, is Cream Sherry, first developed in Bristol, England. The widespread success of Harvey's Bristol Cream notwithstanding, Cream Sherry (even Harvey's) can be an enjoyable after-dinner drink.
- **Fino:** This is both the general name of the unfinished flor Sherries and the name of one of the finished products within that group. This Sherry is pale, dry, and best served chilled as an apéritif in the hot summer.
- **Manzanilla:** This is a pale, dry, fino Sherry that comes from the coastal town of Sanlúcar de Barrameda. Because it matures in casks stored near the sea, it acquires a tangy, salty flavor from the coastal air. Serve it with tapas.
- **Oloroso:** Like Fino Sherry, Oloroso Sherry is both the name of a category of Sherries—those unaffected by

flor—and the name of one of the finished products in this category. There is a popular perception that darker Sherries are, by definition, sweeter. This is not so, however. Oloroso Sherry itself is, in its natural state, quite dry. Good Oloroso is richly flavored, full-bodied, and medium-brown in color.

RECOMMENDED SHERRY PRODUCERS

Domecq	Osborne
Emilio Lustau	Savory & James
González Byass	

Other Fortified Wines

Whereas Port and Sherry are generally enjoyed as beverages, Madeira and Marsala are more commonly used for cooking. If you find that you enjoy Sherry and Port, you might want to experiment with these.

Madeira

Madeira is a small Portuguese-governed island in the Atlantic Ocean off the northwest coast of Africa. The most common of the eponymous fortified wines that it produces are used for cooking, but the better ones are consumed as cocktails. The early American colonists used to drink Madeira, so the island has a long history of producing and exporting its goods. Madeira is heated during the production process. It was discovered that heat improved the taste of the wine in the 1600s when Madeira was shipped across the Atlantic in hot cargo ships.

Light brown in color, Madeira can be sweet or dry. The four primary types of Madeira are:

- **Bual:** rich and raisiny
- **Malmsey:** a British corruption of Malvasia, a grape variety; the sweetest Madeira
- **Sercial:** the driest and most acidic Madeira
- **Verdelho:** medium-dry

The best Madeira is often aged for many decades and is a rare treat. If you don't see one of these four names on the bottle, you are getting an inferior quality Madeira. Think you're ready to venture into the world of Madeira wines? Start exploring this variety by comparing a pale Sercial to a dark Malmsey to figure out which style you like best.

RECOMMENDED MADEIRA PRODUCERS

Colombo	Veiga França
Cossart Gordon	Blandy's

Marsala

Named for the town on the western tip of Sicily, Marsala is a brown-colored fortified wine made from the green-skinned Catarrato grape, a local variety. After harvesting, the grapes are dried prior to fermentation, which raises the sugar level. After fortification, Marsala is often sweetened and darkened with grape juice syrup. Barrel-aging mellows its flavors. Of all the fortified wines, Marsala is the least distinctive as a beverage and is best kept in the kitchen. Marsala comes in two styles, dry and sweet.

RECOMMENDED MARSALA PRODUCERS

Florio	Pelligrino
Lombardo	Rallo

Kosher Wine

To be kosher, wine must be made by strictly Sabbath-observing Jews, although they might well be advised by professional winemakers who have never visited any house of worship. Additionally, kosher wine must not be produced from young vines, and, in Israel, the vineyards must lie fallow (unused) for one harvest every seven years. Wine can be labeled "kosher for Passover" to indicate that it has not come into contact with bread or leavened dough products, and those labeled *mevushal* kosher have been boiled, rendering it useless for pagan rituals while ensuring that it remains kosher after being touched or served by a non-Jew. This boiling sounds like a harsh process, but one particular Burgundy *Grand Cru*, Château Corton Grancey, is famously pasteurized every vintage without any negative effect. (Legendary kosher winemaker Baron Herzog cleverly obtained permission from a rabbinical council to bring his *mevushal* wines to the boiling point of alcohol, significantly lower than that of water.)

So kosher wine, like nonkosher wine, can come in any imaginable style and range, from inexpensive to world-class great. And yet, many of us share a preconceived notion of what kosher wine tastes like . . . grapey and sweet. It is important to remember that there is not a single mention in the Old Testament, not in any Book, of the Concord grape.

The Origins of American Kosher Wine

Jewish immigrants came to the United States from Europe in several waves during the early twentieth century, and New York City was their usual port of entry. With the

Californian wine industry still toddling and imports still uncommon, it fell to the local wineries in and around New York to produce the kosher wine necessary for observing the Sabbath and holidays. The native Concord grape of the species *Vitis labrusca* thrived in the nearby vineyards where many European varieties previously died in infancy, and so this hardy and abundant grapevine became the primary source of American kosher wine.

A distant cousin of European *Vitis vinifera*, the Concord grape (named for the town in Massachusetts, where it was first cultivated) is more suitable for the manufacture of grape jelly than for winemaking. The aroma of wine made from Concord and other *labrusca* grapes is often described as "foxy," a wine term as derogatory as it is vague. "Foxiness," we now know, indicates the presence of certain compounds (methyl anthranilate and o-aminoacetophenone) unique to the *labrusca* grapes native to the Eastern Seaboard.

"Foxiness" isn't as unpleasant as most wine snobs like to suggest. You might wonder how strange the great European wines would taste to palates honed on centuries of refined *labrusca* viticulture, if such a thing existed. But North America is without such a tradition, and so the early Jewish immigrants in and around New York City fashioned an acceptable wine from the local vines by mitigating Concord's rank grapiness and enamel-stripping acidity with liberal doses of sugar.

Thus, after a few generations, this has become the accepted traditional style of kosher wine in America. And although many wines in the world could be made as kosher for Passover, the sweet and "foxy " fruit of the Concord vine, more akin to cough syrup than to fine wine, remains a sentimental favorite among Jewish Americans.

Other Types of Kosher Wine

Kosher wine doesn't have to be made from the native North American Concord grape that has become such a part of Jewish tradition. Today, kosher wines are made in California, France, Italy, and Israel, using "normal" wine grapes like the Cabernet Sauvignon and Chenin Blanc. The history of ceremonial wine in all cultures is one rich in red wine, with little or no attention paid to whites. That is still true today, but kosher whites do exist. The best introduction to good kosher wines are the Baron Herzog wines from California. They are good and widely available (by kosher wine standards).

The Kedem winery in upstate New York still produces Concord grape–based kosher wines. If you want a traditional red Concord wine that doesn't have sugar added to it, look for the Kedem Concord Natural. If you are looking for a very sweet wine, then Kedem Malaga is a logical choice.

Organic Wine

It was only a matter of time before the organic movement reached the vineyards. Most winemakers are farmers. The wines they produce will be only as good as the grapes they grow. So they have a natural interest in growing the best-tasting fruit and maintaining the health of the land for years to come.

Conventional Versus Organic Farming

Organic farming forsakes chemicals in favor of more "natural" techniques. From a practical viewpoint this means that organic farmers will:

- Fertilize using composted animal manure or algae.
- Combat weeds by mowing them periodically and allowing them to rot back into the ground, providing organic fertilizer.
- Get rid of insects by growing other plants in the vineyard to attract "beneficial" bugs to act as predators.

Organic farming is as much philosophy as practice. The objective is balance in nature and the long-term health of the soil, the plants, and, ultimately, the wine drinker. Grapes grown in this fashion can be government certified as organic grapes. The wine can then be advertised as wine from "organically grown grapes." The irony is that many producers are using organic techniques because they make good sense—but not seeking certification because of the rigidity of government oversight.

Conventional Versus Organic Winemaking

The term *organic*—or, more precisely, the government certification of a wine as "organic"—doesn't stop at the harvest. Organic winemakers have to use only approved organic methods in cellar operations as well. The subject of organic has been muddied over the practice of adding sulfur dioxide (sulfites), which is the main ingredient wineries use to extend the shelf life of wine.

The health effects of sulfites are negligible except for a small percentage of people who have a sensitivity. It's difficult to make a wine that will keep for any length of time without adding some sulfites to those that are naturally produced by the yeasts during fermentation. But to be able to call a wine "organic," the winemaker has to abide by strict, government-mandated sulfite rules.

How to Know You're Getting "Organic"

Organic claims on store shelves are just plain confusing. When you want an organic alternative to conventional wine, who and what should you believe? The answer is on the label—if you understand what the terms mean. There are four categories that organic wines can claim:

- **100 Percent Organic.** The wine must be from 100 percent organically produced ingredients. There can be no added sulfites. It can have naturally occurring sulfites from fermentation, but they have to measure less than 100 parts per million.
- **Organic.** The wine must be from 95 percent organic ingredients. The nonorganic 5 percent has to be either an agricultural ingredient that's not organically available or another substance like added yeast. There can be no added sulfites, but naturally occurring sulfites can measure up to 100 parts per million.
- **Made with Organic Ingredients/Organic Grapes/ Organically Grown Grapes.** The wine must be from 70 percent organic ingredients. Sulfites have to measure below 100 parts per million.
- **Some Organic Ingredients.** The wine has less than 70 percent organic ingredients. The label can't have any information about a certifying agency or any other reference to organic content.

Simply put, "organic" wines are made from certified organic grapes and contain no additives such as sulfites. Wineries that use organic grapes but add sulfites or other additives can only be labeled "made with organically grown grapes."

RECOMMENDED CERTIFIED ORGANIC WINE PRODUCERS

Frey Vineyards	Cooper Mountain Vineyards
Badger Mountain Vineyard	Organic Wine Works
Bonterra Vineyards	

Vegetarian and Vegan Wine

Winemakers—both organic and nonorganic—often use animal-based products in the fining process to clarify the wine. The fining agents act as magnets to attract the unwanted material, which falls to the bottom of the tank. The clear wine is siphoned off, but trace amounts of the fining agent may linger in the finished wine.

Wines suitable for vegans use earth-based fining agents such as bentonite clay, food-grade diatomaceous earth, carbon, and kaolin (similar to bentonite). But the fining agents aren't listed on the label, and you have to do some investigating. It's not that vegan wines are scarce. There are lots of them. They're just not always advertised as vegan. However, as veganism gains popularity, some wineries are making it clear that their wines don't use animal products. A quick Internet search for "vegan wine" will bring up various sites that list wines suitable for vegans.

A word to the wise vegan: A suitable wine in one vintage may not be suitable in the next. Winemakers can change their fining agents from one year to the next. You might have to make a call to the producer or exporter to find out. A simpler solution to finding a vegan-friendly wine is to look for wines labeled "unfined."

Filtering is another process to remove impurities. A wine can be both fined and filtered, it can undergo one process without the other, or it can undergo neither. "Unfined" on the label means that no clarifying agent has been used.

CHAPTER 3

How Is Wine Made?

Although winemaking has been raised to a fine art and an increasingly precise science over the last five thousand years, it remains, in essence, a relatively simple process. Wine grapes, *Vitis vinifera*, can grow with considerable ease in most warm-to-temperate climates. Ripe grapes contain a solution of natural sugar and water, with more sugar than in most other fruits. Additionally, the skin of the grape is an ideal medium for the accumulation of natural yeasts. These one-celled plants consume the natural sugar and convert it to ethyl alcohol and carbon dioxide, which, as it escapes the fermenting vat, protects the must from harmful oxidation. Had we not evolved into humans, it's almost conceivable that apes could have learned to make wine—it's that simple. Of course, in the thousands of years since this process was first observed, technology has played an ever-increasing role in winemaking.

There are many technological options available to the modern winemaker. Equipment such as crushers, destemmers, and fermentation tanks come in so many shapes and varieties that each and every winery in the world might well have a unique configuration of them. However, whether the end product is red, white, or pink, and whether it is cheap or expensive, there are several principles common to all winemaking.

Combating Oxidation

First of all, air is the enemy. Exposure to oxygen robs wine of its fresh-tasting qualities and also encourages the activity of acetobacter, the naturally occurring microbes that consume ethyl alcohol and eventually convert it into acetic acid (vinegar). It is an ironic twist of nature that while grapes virtually seek to become wine, wine in turn aspires to become vinegar—again, with minimal effort. The winemaker, therefore, must take care to prevent air from ruining the wine. These precautions begin in the fields at harvest time.

It is crucial that the grapes are picked and transported to the winery without prematurely splitting the skins. While handpicking is best, mechanical harvesting machines have been developed, and these can handle grape bunches with sufficient care. A judicious sprinkling of powdered sulfur dioxide ("sulfite"), an effective antioxidant, is often applied to protect harvested grapes on their way to the winery.

Exposure to air is also minimized during fermentation, and nature lends a helping hand in this stage of winemaking. The carbon dioxide that is discharged by the yeasts, along with ethyl alcohol, provides a cushion of protection against the ambient air. This is especially important in the fermentation of red wine, which usually takes place in an open vat.

As a final precaution against the ill effects of exposure to air, many inexpensive wines are pasteurized—that is, heated to a high enough temperature to kill the acetobacter. This is an effective way at least to delay the effects of oxidation, and it is the reason why jug wines enjoy such a long shelf life after opening. Inevitably, however, if the wine is kept too long, a new wave of acetobacter will find its way into the wine and begin the process of vinegar-making once again. Because pasteurization is a harsh process that prevents the long-term evolution of wine in the bottle (some oxidation is actually beneficial), this process is rarely used for high-quality wines. A famous exception is Château Corton Grancey, a *Grand Cru* red from France's Burgundy region.

Through the Glass, Clearly

Clarity is another goal common to all winemaking, and the brilliant transparency of both red and white wines does not come naturally. Wine is, by nature, cloudy with dead yeast and tiny particulate matter. Several processes, including fining, centrifuging, filtration, racking, and cold stabilization, may be used to clarify wine.

Fining

Fining is one of the few processes in which foreign matter is introduced into the wine. Whipped egg whites have long been used as a fining agent for quality wines. Shortly after fermentation is complete, the wine is transferred to a large settling tank. When added to the tank of young, unfinished wine, the mass of whipped egg whites slowly sinks to the bottom, electrostatically attracting undesirable particles along the way. The clear wine is then drawn off, leaving the coagulated meringue at the bottom of the barrel. In addition to egg whites, casein (milk protein) and bentonite clay (aluminum silicate) can also be used as fining agents.

Centrifuging and Filtration

These are two quick and effective methods of clarifying wine. To centrifuge wine, a container of unfinished, cloudy wine is rapidly rotated so that heavy particles are separated from the wine by centrifugal force. Unfortunately, this process tends to strip wine of some desirable qualities as well, and centrifuging is being used less and less frequently for quality wines. Filtration is the simple and straightforward process of screening out unwanted particles from the wine by passing it through layers of filter paper or synthetic fiber mesh. Though less harsh than centrifuging, there are some fine wines with the term "unfiltered" on the label—the implication being that filtration also strips wine of some desirable qualities.

Racking

Compared to fining, centrifuging, and filtrating, the process of racking is a relatively passive means of clarifying wine. Racking works for the same reason as centrifuging: Unwanted particles are heavier than the wine itself and will eventually sink to the bottom if the wine is left undisturbed. The clear wine can then be "racked," that is, drawn off to another barrel. Again, air is the enemy, and unwanted exposure to air during the racking process must be avoided. Red wines in particular, which are often held for many months in the barrel prior to bottling, may undergo multiple rackings.

Cold Stabilization

This is a relatively harsh treatment used to clarify inexpensive wines. This process involves chilling a tank of wine almost to the freezing point. At this low temperature, minerals such as potassium tartrate (cream of tartar) become less soluble and precipitate out as crystals. Have you ever seen "wine crystals" on a cork? Though often mistaken for unwanted sediment, this accumulation of wine crystals is actually a good sign—it means that the wine has not been cold-stabilized, which would have eliminated the crystals prior to bottling.

Differences Between White Wine and Red Wine Production

Although the prevention of oxidation and some process of clarification are common to all winemaking, there are fundamental differences between the production of red wine and that of white wine. In short, white wine is fermented grape juice—that is, the juice is extracted from the grapes prior to fermentation. Red wine, however, is the juice of fermented grapes, which are crushed into a thick mush—the "must"—from which the juice is extracted after fermentation. Interestingly, the finest rosés are often produced from red grapes handled like white grapes: The red grape skins, which provide color, are removed prior to fermentation, leaving only a slight blush of color in the wine.

The differences between the production of red wine and that of white wine begin in the vineyards. Most of the classic red-wine grape varieties—for example, Cabernet Sauvignon, Merlot, and Syrah—thrive in climates warmer than those that are ideal for the important white-wine varieties. Full ripeness is so crucial for red-wine grapes because the essential components of quality red wine—rich fruit flavors, tannin, body, and color—develop in the grape in the final stage of ripening. However, these grapes must not ripen too quickly. If that happens, the resulting wine often lacks depth and harmony of flavors. The longer the growing season, the more complex the wine, and a prolonged growing season that doesn't bring the grapes to full ripeness until early autumn is ideal. Although most of sunny California's vineyards are planted in the warm valleys, the finest California reds usually come from grapes grown on the cooler slopes overlooking the valleys.

High-quality red and white grapes can often grow side by side, but in general the important white varieties perform best in climates too cool for great reds. Chardonnay, Sauvignon Blanc, and especially Riesling grapes tend to make uninteresting, low-acid wines in the same climates in which the great red grapes may thrive. But Chardonnay is made into the great white wine of the chilly Chablis region of France, an area whose red grapes rarely mature fully. Germany's Rieslings are among the finest wines in the world, yet German red wines are of little more than curiosity value. Riesling, along with an increasing amount of Chardonnay, have been the only *Vitis vinifera* varieties that regularly succeed in upstate New York, where winter can be brutally cold.

Although the climates in which red and white-wine grapes thrive may vary, the cultivation techniques are not very different. The real differences between red and white wine production begin after harvest.

White Wine

As soon as possible after picking, white-wine grapes are fed into a crushing and/or destemming machine that gently splits the skins. For most white wines, prolonged skin contact after crushing is not desirable, so the skins and other grape matter are quickly separated from the juice. However, in making some of the great white wines of the world, the skins are allowed to remain in the juice for a day or so in order to lend additional body and character to the wine. A juicing machine uses pressurized sulfur dioxide gas to squeeze out the juice, which then goes to a settling tank, where undesirable solids such as dirt and seeds settle to the bottom. The juice might be centrifuged at this stage, but, as previously mentioned, the centrifuge can remove the good with the bad. The clarified white grape juice is now ready for fermentation . . . well, almost.

Some doctoring of the grape juice might be deemed necessary by the winemaker. Although regulations vary around the world, adjustments in acid and sugar levels are often called for. In cooler regions, where even white-wine grape varieties struggle to achieve full ripeness, sugar may be added to the juice, through a process called "chaptalization." Without enough sugar, the wine might not attain the desired alcohol level. Fully ripened grapes usually ferment to an alcohol content of 12 percent by volume. The acidity might also be adjusted at this point. Calcium carbonate may be added to reduce acidity, whereas tartaric or other acids may be added to raise it. In the final analysis, the sugar and acid must be in balance at the desired levels in order to make good wine. Now fermentation can begin.

Fermentation: Grapes Become Wine

Although wild wine yeast naturally accumulates on grape skins during the growing season, almost all winemakers prefer to control fermentation and, therefore, introduce carefully cultivated yeast to the juice. Fermentation proceeds slowly, it is hoped, because a rapid fermentation might raise the temperature to a level that kills the yeast. Also, the yeast itself imparts character to the wine, so a slow fermentation, which allows longer contact with the yeast, is desirable. Most winemakers control the temperature of the fermentation by refrigeration and recirculation. The carbon dioxide that is produced during fermentation is permitted to escape from the enclosed vat without allowing ambient air back in—yet another precaution against oxidation.

Through this process, the white grape juice has become white wine—rough, unfinished wine that still needs some tinkering, including a filtration to remove any remaining sugar and particles. Just prior to fining, the winemaker may deem it necessary to add some sweet, unfermented grape juice in which the yeasts and acetobacters have been killed. This is done to add roundness to the flavor and to take the acidic edge off a harsh-tasting wine. However, the new wine has its own way of reducing its acidity: malolactic fermentation.

This process, like alcoholic fermentation, occurs naturally but is usually controlled by the winemaker. In the spring following the harvest, warm weather activates microbes in the wine that convert malic acid into lactic acid and carbon dioxide. Malic acid, which is naturally present in apples, is sharply acidic. Lactic acid, which develops naturally in dairy products, is only half as acidic as malic acid. Thus, malolactic fermentation softens a wine's acidity profile. This process can be controlled by the winemaker to such a degree that you can find a range of wines in the market that have undergone various degrees of malolactic fermentation: from clean, crisp white wines that have not undergone any malolactic fermentation; to soft, fleshy white wines that have undergone full malolactic fermentation; to wines somewhere in the middle, a blend of wines made in the two different styles. Some wines have been known to undergo an unintended malolactic fermentation after bottling, resulting in a funny tasting wine with an unwelcome trace of fizziness.

A Hint or More of Oak

Up until a few decades ago, oak casks were the most economical storage vessels available. Oak imparts distinct flavors to a wine, mainly vanilla and tannin. These flavors are more apparent in white wines than in heavier, more complex reds. Because of the long history of wine storage in oak, these flavors have become accepted as basic components of wine. It is even likely that the style of certain wines, notably the Chardonnay-based white Burgundy wines, evolved in such a way that oak flavors are a necessary and expected facet of the wine's flavor; without oak, such wines might taste incomplete. Now that less expensive storage vessels are available, such as those made of stainless steel, oak flavor is an additive of sorts. In fact, some producers of inexpensive wines circumvent the great expense of oak barrels by adding oak chips to wine held in stainless-steel tanks.

Virtually all wines benefit from a resting period after fermentation and clarification. A few months of aging, either in oak or steel, allows the flavor components in white wine to become more harmonious. Likewise, a resting period in the bottle is beneficial. An unfortunate consequence of the wine boom is that most wines are consumed long before they are at their best. Although red wines generally undergo a much more gradual evolution in the bottle than do white wines, a well-made white wine can improve for five or more years in the bottle. Chardonnays and Rieslings are known to age more gracefully than other white wines.

Red Wine

Red wine is not necessarily "better" than white wine, but well-made red wines have more flavor components and, thus, are typically more complex than white wines. Enjoyable white wine has a prominent acidity profile counterbalanced with a hint of sweetness, restrained fruit flavors, and maybe a touch of oak. That is why white wines are best served chilled—acidic beverages, such as lemonade, taste better at lower temperatures. If served warm, both lemonade and white wine are less enjoyable because the prominent acidity becomes unpleasantly sharp at higher temperatures. Although red wine may be nearly as acidic as white, red wine usually has a wider range of fruit flavors as well as a noticeable amount of tannin, qualities best appreciated at warmer temperatures. The difference is skin-deep.

Whereas (almost) all grapes contain the same greenish pulp, the skins of red-wine grapes give red wine its color, tannins, and assorted fruit flavors. So white grape skins, which add little to white wine, are removed early in the winemaking process, but red grape skins are kept in the fermenting vat for an extended period of time. It is, therefore, necessary to remove the stalks from red-wine grapes as they are crushed, lest the stalks impart excessive tannins on the wine. "Tannins"—the family of organic acids present in grape skins as well as seeds—cause the dry and bitter sensation in your mouth after you bite a grape seed.

The image of half-naked men stomping grapes in an open vat is familiar to many of us. Although technology has replaced the human foot in most corners of the wine world, the open vat is still widely used for red-wine production because grape skins tend to rise to the top of the fermenting must, forming a "cap" atop the juice. In order to extract the desirable qualities from the skins, this cap must be continuously mixed back into the juice. This can be accomplished by pumping juice from the bottom of the barrel over the cap (called "pumping over") or by manually punching the cap back into the juice with a special paddle (called "punched-cap fermentation"). It is said that a punched-cap wine reflects the physical character of the winemaker—a big, strong winemaker will force more extract from the skins, resulting in a big, strong wine. As in white-wine production, temperature control is important, though red wines benefit from a fermentation temperature a little higher than that which is ideal for whites.

Drawing Off the Wine

After fermentation is complete, perhaps one to three weeks later, the new wine is drawn from the fermenting vat, leaving the skins behind. This first run of juice, called "free-run" juice, comes forth voluntarily; forcibly squeezing the juice from the must would extract excessive tannin. Only after the free-run juice is removed is the remaining must squeezed, yielding "press wine," a portion of which might be blended with the free-run juice in order to adjust the tannin level carefully. The wine is then clarified in much the same manner as white wine and transferred to aging barrels, where it can slowly mature. Racking may be necessary every few months if the wine is held in the cellar for a length of time. Prolonged barrel aging before bottling is desirable for most types of red wine, since the broad array of flavor components generally needs more time to harmonize in red wines than in white wines.

Many wines, both red and white, are blends of several different grapes. Even in the case of wines made entirely from one variety, a winemaker may blend different "lots" (separate barrels) of wine in order to make the best possible wine. The "recipe" for such wines may vary from year to year, depending on the characteristics of the available lots in a given vintage.

When wine is deemed ready for release, it is transferred to bottles in a mechanized process notable for its sanitation.

Once again, air is the enemy, and care is taken not to allow its contact with the wine during bottling. Germs and impurities are also mortal enemies, and the bottling process is often the most highly mechanized step in the entire operation, as sparkling-clean bottles are filled, corked, capped, and labeled with minimal human contact. For the finest wines, it is often advantageous for the winery to then keep the bottles in storage for two or more years. This makes for better wine when it finally reaches the market, and in many cases the value of the wine will have increased greatly during its slumber.

PART 2

The Wine Universe

CHAPTER 4

Varietal Wines

As you walk through your favorite wine store, you'll notice that wines are often organized by country of origin. For classic regions like France, wines may be organized into smaller regions such as Bordeaux, Burgundy, and the Rhône. Red wines and whites may be in separate sections. Many stores will organize their wines by varietal. Sparkling wines will likely be in a separate section altogether. Rare and expensive wines are often located in a specially designated, climate-controlled room. Why are wines divided up this way? What are varietal wines? Read on to find out.

The Region-Versus-Variety Debate

As you shop for wine, pay attention to the fact that some wines are labeled by grape variety (such as Merlot and Chardonnay), while others are labeled with place names (such as Pomerol and Pouilly-Fuissé). Why is this so?

Old-World Distinctions

Perhaps because every inch of European soil has long been spoken for, European *vignerons* have historically placed primary importance on the geographic origin of wine rather than its grape variety. Long before quality wine was produced all over the world, the many centuries of trial and error had already helped wine producers in France, Italy, Germany, and elsewhere in Europe to match the best-suited *vinifera* grape variety with its proper venue. French winemakers found, for instance, that Cabernet Sauvignon could ripen beautifully in a warm, sunny autumn in the Médoc, while Pinot Noir ripened at its own ideal pace in the cooler, continental climate of Burgundy. In the Piedmont region of Northern Italy, the Nebbiolo grape became a superstar, one that refuses thus far to perform its magic on any other soil.

Yesterday's experiments have led to today's wine laws, and so most European wine laws now dictate the grape varieties allowed for each region. Thus, when you buy a European bottle, it is usually—although not always—labeled primarily by its geographic origin, and the grape varieties used to make it are stipulated by law. Wine in the New World, however, is a different story.

New-World Differences

California was the first commercially successful outpost for European wine grapes in the New World. In the 1800s, the Golden State not only proved that it could produce high-quality wine occasionally on par with the finest wines of Europe, it also demonstrated a cost effective capacity to produce inexpensive "jug wine" for the immigrant working class, for whom a glass or two of wine with a meal was no more special than coffee with breakfast. What better way to label such wine, it was thought at the time, than with familiar placenames from the old country? Thus, an ocean of Californian "rhine," "chianti," "hock," "burgundy," and "chablis" flowed forth to consumers across America, who were pleased to enjoy an inexpensive wine that was at least as good as the village wine back home.

However, this left the quality-oriented Californian producers in a quandary—place-names like "Calistoga" and "Napa" had little or no meaning to the wine connoisseur, yet co-opting a high-end placename such as "Margaux" would be both unseemly and deceiving. The solution was to label by the grape variety used to make the wine, to better demonstrate that a "choice" variety—such as the Cabernet Sauvignon grape responsible for great wines of Bordeaux—was used in pure form to produce the wine. Thus, "varietal" labeling was born.

In contrast to the many centuries of trial and error that led to the development of European wine laws, there has been a relatively short period of experimentation in the New World. Wine producers in California, the Pacific Northwest, Australia, South America, and elsewhere are constantly planting new grape varieties in relatively young wine regions. Therefore, it would make little or no sense to label a red wine simply "Napa Valley," where a half-dozen different premium red varieties are cultivated.

The Current Lay of the Land

Walk into almost any wine store today and you will find wines sorted by both grape variety and geographic origin. There will most likely be a "French" section, perhaps further divided into "Rhône," "Burgundy," and "Bordeaux" subsections. The Californian wines will be in a separate section altogether, and the wines from Australia in still another part of the store. And yet, you will find wine made from the Syrah grape in all three areas—Hermitage from France, Shiraz from Australia, and varietal Syrah from California. Ditto for wines made from Chardonnay, Sauvignon Blanc, and many other grapes. This doesn't happen in the grocery store, where oranges from Florida and California are found side by side, rather than in opposite ends of the produce section. That's because an orange is an orange, and the difference between Californian and Floridian oranges is negligible compared to the difference between Californian oranges and the lemons grown in an adjacent grove. And so while your local wine merchant might find it expedient to arrange his store by geographical origin, it would probably be more useful for the wine consumer if the wine store (and the rest of the wine universe) were organized according to grape variety.

Today's wine drinker appears to be learning to love wine one grape at a time. Cabernet Sauvignon and Chardonnay, arguably the king and queen of Napa Valley grapes, were the favorites of Californian fans in the 1970s. Then Merlot became wildly popular after the release of scientific research suggesting that red wine offered healthful properties, which convinced many white wine drinkers to change colors. Now Syrah is the flavor of the day, and wine consumers are greeting the worldwide profusion of fine Syrah/Shiraz–based wines with considerable enthusiasm. Of course, all wines, Syrah, Merlot, or otherwise, have to come from somewhere. Yet, with few exceptions, the modern wine consumer is primarily buying wine according to the grape variety, not the region of origin.

Varietal Wines, Grape by Grape

Unless labeled otherwise as "pear wine," "blueberry wine," or something else, it is safe to assume from the label on a bottle that "wine" is produced from grapes. There are many species of grapes, however, and grape varieties vary greatly in color and character, as well as in winemaking potential. Most of the world's wines come from the *Vitis vinifera* species, the classic European grape family whose vines were first brought to America prior to the American Revolution. Due to the *phylloxera* vine pest, however, the *vinifera* vines didn't produce much wine in the New World for more than a century. Instead, early American wine came from a variety of other grape species, including the East Coast's native *Vitis labrusca* grapes; the Ohio River Valley's *Vitis riparia* species; and the *Vitis rotundifolia* grape species. The Scuppernong grape of the American Southeast, thought to be the first native grape that American settlers tried to turn into wine, is a member of this last species.

Vitis labrusca's most famous family member is the Concord grape. Although presently it is not given much serious consideration by the wine world, decent wine can be coaxed from it, as long as enough sugar is added to mitigate Concord's enamel-stripping acidity. Generally, these grapes are used to make grape juice and grape jelly rather than wine, although there is a century-old tradition of producing cloyingly sweet kosher wine from the Concord grape. Other *labrusca* grapes used more in the past than in American winemaking today are the Catawba, Delaware, and Niagara varieties. The biggest contribution that native North American grapes have made to the wine world is to provide rootstock for *vinifera* vines. Many of the *vinifera* vines around the world today are grafted onto *Vitis riparia* vine roots, which are resistant to the destructive *phylloxera* vine louse.

The *vinifera* family of grapes, which come in red-, black-, and green-skinned varieties, is used to make the vast majority of the world's wine. There are hundreds of *vinifera* grape varieties, but only a few dozen of these—generally called "aromatic" varieties—are suitable for wine production. Of these, only a few are used to produce the world's finest wines. These "noble grape varieties" include Cabernet Sauvignon, Pinot Noir, Merlot, Syrah, Sangiovese, and Nebbiolo among the red wine grapes, as well as the white wine grapes Riesling, Chardonnay, and Sauvignon Blanc.

Varietal wines—those labeled and sold according to the grape variety from which they are made—must meet government-mandated minimum varietal percentages. In other words, there is a minimum percentage of a wine that must be made from the grape variety indicated on the label for it to be labeled as such. Although the label on your bottle may say Chardonnay, there is a very good chance that the wine is a blend made from Chardonnay and other grapes. However, these minor-percentage grapes are usually not credited on the bottle.

Why are varietal wines so popular? Because the grape variety used to make the wine is the single most important determinant of the wine's flavor. The "aromatic" grape varieties are just that—they impart a recognizable set of aromas and flavors to wine.

Following is a breakdown of the most common and popular grape varieties.

Wine Wisdom

A wine is described as "varietally correct" if the grape variety is easily discernable from the aroma and taste of the wine. Although wine made from a particular grape variety will also display traits associated with its geographical origin, there are certain qualities we have come to associate with the most common grape varieties no matter where they are produced.

Red Wine Grapes

Cabernet Sauvignon

Main growing regions: Bordeaux (France), Australia, California, Washington State, Chile, and Tuscany (Italy)
Aromas and flavors: Black currants, green peppers, chocolate, and mint
Acidity: Moderate
Tannin: Moderate to prominent
Body: Medium to full
Major mixing partners: Sangiovese (Tuscany), Merlot (Bordeaux), Shiraz (Australia)

Cabernet Sauvignon is perhaps the noblest red variety of all. Although its precise origins are unknown, Cabernet Sauvignon first became noteworthy as a grape variety in Bordeaux in the late 1700s. Today, this variety is at or near the top of every connoisseur's great red varietal list. Appearing either alone or in combination with other grape varieties, Cabernet Sauvignon generally makes rich, tannic wines capable of commanding high prices. The most expensive and well made of these often need a few years of aging in order to display their fine qualities fully—multiple layers of fruit flavors and a smooth but firm tannic structure. Cabernet Sauvignon benefits from contact with new oak, which lends balance and further complexity.

There are several exquisite versions of Cabernet Sauvignon from California, particularly from the Napa Valley, that are not blended with other grapes. One of the most famous and expensive of these is Heitz Cellar "Martha's Vineyard" Cabernet Sauvignon. President Ronald Reagan proudly served the 1974 vintage of this wine to the president of France at a state dinner. Many top California wine producers have recently begun to combine Cabernet Sauvignon with other grapes that offer complementary flavors.

As a blending grape, Cabernet Sauvignon successfully shares a bottle with Syrah (Shiraz) in wines from Australia, and with Sangiovese in "super-Tuscan" wines from Italy. In Bordeaux, Cabernet Sauvignon is usually blended with a combination of Merlot, Cabernet Franc (one of its parent grapes), Malbec, and/or Petit Verdot. It is this Bordeaux blend that has found favor in California. As mentioned earlier, because United States law requires a minimum of 75 percent of a particular grape variety to qualify for varietal labeling, the California wine industry coined the term "Meritage," to distinguish these fine blended wines from ordinary table wines that similarly do not qualify for varietal labeling.

In any wine shop, you might find varietal Cabernet Sauvignon from Chile, Australia, California, Washington State, Italy, Spain, or France. Expensive as great Cabernet Sauvignon can be, the bargains are out there. Look for varietal wines from the South of France (labeled "vin de pays d'Oc," the "country wine" from the Languedoc) and also from Chile. The Cabernet/Shiraz blends from Australia are often excellent values as well.

The finest and most sought-after versions of Cabernet Sauvignon come from several different places.

- **California:** There are a handful of ultra-expensive, reserve Cabernet Sauvignons and Meritage wines from the Napa Valley, including the previously mentioned Heitz Cellar "Martha's Vineyard," Screaming Eagle, Caymus Special Selection, Harlan Estate, Opus One, Rubicon Estate, and Phelps "Insignia."
- **Australia:** From Penfold's comes the noteworthy Cabernet Sauvignon Bin 707.
- **Italy:** "Super-Tuscan" reds from coastal Tuscany include Antinori's "Solaia," a blend of 90 percent Cabernet Sauvignon and 10 percent Sangiovese.
- **Chile:** Although not yet available, there is good reason to expect super-premium Cabernet Sauvignon from this region in the near future.

Suggested Food Pairings

The assertive flavors of Cabernet Sauvignon—young or old—match nicely with lamb, beef, and other red meat dishes. Young Cabernet Sauvignon is especially well paired with meats from the grill because the youthful fruit flavors are a perfect counterpoint to the pleasantly bitter scorch imparted by the open fire.

It is in the Bordeaux subregions of Médoc and Graves, however, where the world's most elegant, age-worthy, and expensive Cabernet Sauvignon–based wines are produced. Two of the top-rated Bordeaux châteaux, Château Mouton Rothschild and Château Latour, rely on Cabernet Sauvignon for 70 percent of their blends. These and other highly rated Bordeaux châteaux produce wines that can age well for many decades and command hundreds of dollars for a bottle from a great year.

Recommended Cabernet Sauvignon		
Name	**Region**	**Price**
Niebaum-Coppola Claret	California	$
J. Lohr "Seven Oaks"	Paso Robles, CA	$
Viña Montes "Alpha"	Curicó Valley, Chile	$
Chateau St. Jean	Sonoma, CA	$$
Woodward Canyon "Artist Series"	Columbia Valley, Washington	$$
Château Lynch-Bages 1998	Pauillac, Bordeaux	$$$
Pine Ridge "Stags Leap"	Napa Valley, CA	$$$
Ornellaia 1999	Bolgheri, Tuscany, Italy	$$$$
Château Mouton Rothschild 1998	Pauillac, Bordeaux	$$$$

Pinot Noir

Main growing regions: Burgundy (France), California, and Oregon
Aromas and flavors: Cherries, raspberries, soil, cola, and smoke
Acidity: Moderate to high
Tannin: Low to moderate
Body: Light to medium
Major mixing partners: None

If it were not so difficult to grow, Pinot Noir would enjoy a reputation for greatness equal to that of Cabernet Sauvignon. It is the noble red grape of France's Burgundy region where, under ideal conditions, it yields ruby-colored wines with a velvety richness that has seduced wine lovers for centuries. Whereas the outstanding Cabernet Sauvignons of Bordeaux are predictably excellent without generating a lot of unexpected emotion, great Pinot Noirs of Burgundy overwhelm your senses every time with their striking beauty.

Unlike Cabernet Sauvignon, which traveled with ease from Bordeaux to California's warmer valleys, where it thrives in sunshine, Pinot Noir has a harder time in this region. With the exception of a few pockets (such as Santa Barbara, Sonoma Coast, and Carneros), Pinot Noir ripens too quickly on the hot California valley floors and tends to be flat and uninteresting. Pinot Noir seems to be more at home up north in Oregon, however, where the long, cool growing season allows the Pinot Noir fruit flavors to develop slowly.

Perhaps the best use of Pinot Noir grapes in California is as the main component in brut rosé-style, Blanc de Noirs sparkling wines. Several of the great French Champagne houses, in order to meet growing worldwide demand, opened shop in California. Here they found that Pinot Noir, a vital component of Champagne in France, grows to greater ripeness in the California sunshine. More ripeness means more color in the skin, and more fruit flavors as well. When gently pressed and quickly removed from the vat, Pinot Noir skins lend a delightful "blush" of copper color to Champagne-method sparkling wine. In France, such ripeness is quite rare, and brut rosés from the Champagne region are accordingly uncommon and expensive. The better California versions are often an excellent value.

Decent Pinot Noir is never cheap. A good way to get to know this grape is by trying varietal-labeled Pinot Noir from the big, reputable Burgundy (Bourgogne as it's known in France) houses. These will usually be labeled "Bourgogne

Pinot Noir." If you feel like paying for it, move up-market from there to the better red Burgundies, although this region is very difficult (and expensive) to get to know. The Côte Chalonnaise subregion of Burgundy offers two inexpensive and enjoyable Pinot Noir–based wines: Givry and Mercurey.

Many Oregonian interpretations of Pinot Noir are closer in style to their Burgundian brethren than they are to their Californian neighbors. Ask a reliable wine merchant to suggest a varietally correct (yet affordable) Pinot Noir.

Suggested Food Pairings

Less pigmented than most red wine grapes, Pinot Noir wines usually have a brick-orange cast rather than a deep purple color. At its best, Pinot Noir is low in tannin and high in glycerine (hence, the "velvet"), with a lively, acidic backbone that gives length and focus to its typical flavors. Such structure makes Pinot Noir a highly versatile food wine.

Full-bodied red Burgundy from the Côte de Nuits subregion is made entirely from Pinot Noir and is a classic accompaniment to beef roasts. The lighter red Burgundies from the Côte de Beaune are perfect with game birds such as pheasant and partridge and can even pair well with fish dishes. The Pinot Noirs from Oregon can be very Burgundian in structure and range from a light Côte de Beaune style to a richer Côte de Nuits style; they match with food accordingly. The light, clean acidity and modest tannin of typical Pinot Noir makes it suitable with all but the lightest of seafood dishes.

Recommended Pinot Noir

Name	Region	Price
Ramsay	North Coast, CA	$
La Fusina Pinot Nero Langhe Rosso	Dogliani, Piedmont, Italy	$$
Cameron	Dundee, OR	$$
Daniel Rion, Nuits-St.-Georges "Les Grandes Vignes"	Burgundy, France	$$
Siduri "Pisoni Vineyard"	Santa Lucia Highlands, CA	$$
Domaine Drouhin "Cuvée Laurène"	Oregon	$$
Bitouzet-Prieur Volnay "Caillerets" 1999	Burgundy, France	$$$
Domaine Comte Armand, Pommard	Burgundy, France	$$$
Domaine Leroy, Clos de Vougeot 2000	Burgundy, France	$$$$

Merlot

Main growing regions: Bordeaux (France), California, Washington State, Australia, Chile, and Long Island

Aromas and flavors: Plums, currants, blackberries, mocha, and black cherries

Acidity: Low to moderate

Tannin: Low to moderate

Body: Medium

Major mixing partners: Cabernet Sauvignon (Bordeaux)

It is difficult to discuss Merlot without mentioning Cabernet Sauvignon. Just as Cabernet Sauvignon gained recognition in the Médoc subregion of Bordeaux in the late 1700s, so too did Merlot become prominent in the Bordeaux subregions of Pomerol and Saint-Émilion. These two subregions are cooler and wetter than the Médoc, but Merlot can ripen beautifully in these and other climates too cool for Cabernet Sauvignon. The infant wine region on the North Fork of Long Island, for instance, while not quite hot enough for quality Cabernet Sauvignon, shows great promise for Merlot.

Merlot is a distant relative of Cabernet Sauvignon. The biggest difference is that the skin of the Merlot grape is thinner than that of Cabernet Sauvignon; therefore, Merlot is the earlier ripening and less tannic of the two. Merlot has a reputation for making soft, round, and drinkable wines with low acidity and early maturity; yet, according to many experts just a few short years ago, Merlot had no future as a varietal wine in California. In the past few years, however, the Merlot grape has made the transition from being an assistant to Cabernet Sauvignon in blended wines to being a star in its own right. Consequently, it has become a somewhat overrated and misunderstood variety. How did this happen?

When the word got out from the medical journals that red wine was good for your heart, the resulting boom in red-wine sales just about equaled the sales of Beatles records after the rumors of Paul McCartney's death circulated. The wine-drinking public, already hooked on White Zinfandel and Chardonnay, switched *en masse* to red wine. Nonwine drinkers, perhaps mindful of an unpleasant experience with dry, tannic red wine, wanted a supple, drinkable red wine. These consumers turned to Merlot, because of its reputation for low acid and its softness.

California was unprepared for this market shift, with only a few new acres of this variety planted since the mid-1970s. It seems that every winery that was able planted additional Merlot acreage as soon as possible, and the resulting wines were often disappointing. Too often, people buy a Merlot that is shaped more by market forces than by the winemaker's art. These sorts of wines are made out of grapes from very young vines grown at crop levels far too high for fine wine production. It is quite a challenge to find delicious, varietally correct Merlot for under $8.

That being said, there are a few sources of bargains in varietal Merlot. French Merlots labeled "vin de pays d'Oc" are often excellent values, and there are many versions of Merlot available for under $10. South America (Chile and Argentina) produces good, affordable Merlot as well.

What are the characteristics of a good Merlot? Look for rich, plum-like fruit, almost jammy in its concentration, and low levels of acid and tannin. Merlot does not get particularly complex; yet, because of its soft tannin and gentle acidity profile, its pleasing fruit flavors are more accessible than those in sturdier reds.

Suggested Food Pairings

The soft tannin in Merlot also makes it an enjoyable match with a broad variety of foods. Even seafood, especially from the grill, makes a successful pairing with Merlot's unobtrusive flavors. Its somewhat bland personality also allows Merlot to fit nicely with all types of well-seasoned ethnic dishes.

Recommended Merlot

Name	Region	Price
Domaine des Fontanelles	Vin de Pays d'Oc, France	$
Columbia Crest "Grand Estates"	Columbia Valley, WA	$
Blackstone	California	$
Falesco	Umbria, Italy	$
Casa Lapostolle "Cuvée Alexandre"	Rapel Valley, Chile	$
Nelson Estate	Sonoma, CA	$
Raphael	North Fork of Long Island, NY	$$
L'Ecole No. 41	Walla Walla Valley, WA	$$
Beringer "Howell Mountain — Bancroft Ranch"	Napa Valley, CA	$$$
Château Le Bon Pasteur	Pomerol, Bordeaux	$$$

Syrah/Shiraz

Main growing regions: Rhône (France), Australia, and California

Aromas and flavors: Plums, spices, blackberries, and blueberries

Acidity: low to moderate

Tannin: Moderate to prominent

Body: Medium

Major mixing partners: Grenache and Mourvedre (Rhône and Languedoc) and Cabernet Sauvignon (Australia)

The Syrah grape, known as Shiraz in Australia and South Africa, is a noble grape variety held in high esteem by many red-wine lovers. The great and ageworthy wines of the northern Rhône—Hermitage, Côte-Rôtie, Saint-Joseph, and

Cornas—are produced from Syrah. For many years, the finest wine produced in Australia has been Penfolds Grange, and there are of late a handful of other Australian Shiraz–based wines competing for the honor. Australian varietal Shiraz—as well as Shiraz blended with Cabernet Sauvignon—are often remarkable bargains.

California got a late start with this variety. It seems that another grape from the Rhône valley, perhaps the Durif grape, was transplanted by accident instead of Syrah. Today, that grape is known in California as Petite Sirah, and the true Syrah is a relatively recent arrival in California. Some California Syrahs are quite good, but Australia, with a 100-year head start, remains the better source for bargains in Shiraz.

In general, the French version is higher in acid and better with food than the Australian version, which shows more fruit. This is because of the difference in climate. The warmer weather of Australia leads to a more thorough ripening of the grape, which in turn leads to more fruitiness and a lower acidity in the wine. Whereas the French Syrahs tend to display raspberry-like fruit aromas, the Australian versions are often more suggestive of raisins.

Suggested Food Pairings

Many versions of Syrah have a whiff of spiciness, and this dimension of flavor suggests a pairing with exotic seasonings, such as those found in many Asian cuisines.

Petite Sirah, genetically unrelated to the true Syrah, has found a happy home in sunny and hot California. Like Zinfandel, Petite Sirah vines often live to be 100 years old, and "old-vine" versions of Petite Sirah can be beautifully dense, rich, and velvety.

Syrah is, in some ways, the "Next Big Grape." Wine made from Syrah is often a middleweight like Merlot, not heavy like a big, tannic Cabernet Sauvignon, and it grows beautifully in all of the most important wine regions in the world.

Recommended Syrah/Shiraz

Name	Region	Price
Cline	California	$
Woop Woop	Australia	$
Saint Cosme Côtes du Rhône	Rhône, France	$
Jade Mountain	Napa Valley, CA	$$
Errazuriz Reserva	Aconcagua Valley, Chile	$$
Columbia Winery "Red Willow Vineyard"	Woodinville, WA	$$
Isolee Olena IGT	Tuscany, Italy	$$
Rosemount "Balmoral"	McLaren Vale, South Australia	$$$
Guigal Hermitage 2000	Rhône, France	$$$
Penfolds Grange 1998	South Australia	$$$$

Recommended Petite Sirah

Name	Region	Price
Bogle	California	$
Foppiano, Paso Robles	Paso Robles, CA	$
Lolonis "Orpheus"	Redwood Valley, Mendocino, CA	$$
Stag's Leap Vineyard	Stag's Leap, Napa Valley, CA	$$

Zinfandel

Main growing regions: California
Aromas and flavors: Blackberry jam and black pepper
Acidity: Low to moderate
Tannin: Moderate; can be substantial in some versions, light in others
Body: Medium to full
Major mixing partners: Often blended, but rarely credited (California)

This popular grape of unclear origin (recent DNA analysis suggests Eastern Europe) showed up in California in the mid-1800s and has been growing like a weed since then. No other *vinifera* grape thrives as well on Californian heat and sunshine. Unfortunately, the evolution of Zinfandel got sidetracked by the creation of the wildly popular rosé, White Zinfandel, the inspiration for which evolved during a period of slack demand for red wine in the early 1970s.

As a result of this, wine lists must now use the retronym "Red Zinfandel" to indicate the varietal in its original form. Zinfandel is as versatile as it is prolific, capable of a broad range of styles. In addition to White Zinfandel, which is actually a rosé, Zinfandel can range from a light, Beaujolais-like quaff to late-harvest brutes that practically ooze pepper and jammy fruit. Although $5 won't get you a bottle of Zinfandel, $10 bottles do exist, and they are often quite good.

If you suffer sticker shock from a reserve Cabernet Sauvignon or Meritage, opt for an estate-bottled "old vines" Zinfandel ($20 to $30). Its complexity, power, and balance should impress you for the money.

White Zinfandel was wildly popular for a few years after it first reached the market in the early 1970s, and it is still the wine of choice for people who otherwise would not drink wine. The noticeable residual sugar (around 1.5 percent), lower alcohol content (10 percent or so), and fresh strawberry fruit flavor give White Zinfandel its broad appeal. Contrary to what many wine snobs would have you believe, there are several White Zinfandels of quality on the market. The key to good White Zinfandel lies in the color. While many of the palest pink versions are rather bland, the darker versions tend to have more fruit flavors.

Suggested Food Pairings

Zinfandel wines are especially well matched with roasted lamb, other Mediterranean dishes, and even hearty vegetable dishes. Zinfandel stands up well to garlic and powerful seasonings. These buxom, fruity wines are great in a variety of situations, whether alone or with a wine-friendly snack of cheese and crackers.

When it comes to White Zinfandel, there is one particular "match made in heaven" worth noting: White Zinfandel with Thanksgiving dinner. An American holiday deserves an American wine, and the fruitiness and residual sugar of White Zinfandel helps to wash down even the most dried-out turkey breast. Also, because Thanksgiving dinner—turkey and root vegetables, usually—is relatively inexpensive to prepare, White Zinfandel represents an intelligent price matching. Finally, if you celebrate this annual feast with elderly relatives who are not wine buffs, they will probably find White Zinfandel more enjoyable than any other wine.

Recommended Zinfandel/Primitivo

Name	Region	Price
A Mano Primitivo	Apulia, Italy	$
Ravenswood "Vintners Blend"	California	$
Easton, Amador County	Amador, CA	$
Sausal "Family"	Alexander Valley, Sonoma, CA	$
Edmeades	Mendocino, CA	$
Rabbit Ridge "Westside"	Paso Robles, CA	$
Dashe Cellars, Dry Creek	Dry Creek, Sonoma, CA	$$
Howell Mountain Vineyards "Old Vine"	Howell Mountain, Napa Valley, CA	$$

Nebbiolo

Main growing regions: Piedmont (Italy)
Aromas and flavors: Raspberries, mushrooms, plums, leather, and earth
Acidity: Relatively high
Tannin: Prominent in youth, "dusty" with age
Body: Medium
Major mixing partners: None (Some minor, local grapes are blended with Nebbiolo in certain Piedmont wines.)

Named for the dense fogs so prevalent in the vineyards of Piedmont, Italy, the Nebbiolo grape is responsible for several of Italy's—and the world's—finest red wines. The great red wines of Piedmont—Barolo, Barbaresco, Ghemme, Gattinara—are regarded by aficionados as members of the exclusive club of the greatest wines in the world. Nebbiolo grapes have not as yet done well when grown away from their native soil, but somewhere outside of Italy, perhaps, there is a piece of land just waiting to be converted into a great Nebbiolo vineyard. Some growers in California have begun experimenting with Nebbiolo, but they have met with limited success so far.

In the past, the best of these wines, like many Cabernet Sauvignons, were too tannic to drink in their youth and required a decade or so of cellaring. Perhaps more than any other grape variety, Nebbiolo rewards patience. However, more Nebbiolo-based wines are being vinified to be enjoyable in their youth. If you're looking for an affordable way to get to know Nebbiolo, try a Nebbiolo d'Alba or other varietal Nebbiolo from Piedmont selected by a wine merchant or reviewer you trust. Entry level for these wines is $20 or more. If you see one of these wines from a great year such as 1997 or 2000, it might be a bargain, even if it is a little out of your normal price range.

Suggested Food Pairings

Despite their powerful flavors, Barolo and other Nebbiolo-based Italian wines need to be served with food since they are considerably more acidic than equally serious New-World wines. Because the Nebbiolo grape doesn't travel as of yet, it is difficult to abstract out its varietal character from the character of the Piedmontese terroir. No matter—we can still pair food with Nebbiolo without really knowing if we are matching food to the region or the grape. The Italian Nebbiolos are a natural match with rich, earthy dishes such as game and red meat with mushrooms. Even chicken, if prepared in a rustic manner, can hold its own with most of these wines.

Because Nebbiolo has not been transplanted with widespread success from its native Piedmont, it is difficult to differentiate between the characteristics of the grape and those of the region. Look for Piedmont Nebbiolos to be very dry, flavorful but not heavy on the palate, and surprisingly subtle and complex. Watch for the California version, which should become more prevalent in the years ahead, to have stronger plum and raspberry fruit flavors than those from Italy.

Recommended Nebbiolo		
Name	Region	Price
Aurelio Settimo, Langhe Nebbiolo DOC 2000	Piedmont, Italy	$
Produttori del Barbaresco, Barbaresco "Torre" 1998	Piedmont, Italy	$$
Elio Grasso, Barolo "Ginestra Casa Mate" 1998	Piedmont, Italy	$$
Marchesi di Gresy, Barbaresco "Camp Gros" 1998	Piedmont, Italy	$$$
Giacomo Conterno, Barolo "Cascina Francia" 1998	Piedmont, Italy	$$$$
Roberto Voerzio, Barolo "Brunate" 1999	Piedmont, Italy	$$$$

Sangiovese

Main growing regions: Tuscany (Italy), some California
Aromas and flavors: Cherries, raisins, earth, leather, and violets
Acidity: Moderate to high
Tannin: Light to moderate
Body: Light to medium
Major mixing partners: Cabernet Sauvignon (Italy) and Canaiolo Nero (Italy)

Sangiovese is an Italian grape that, like the Nebbiolo, hasn't made a significant impact on the wine world when grown outside of Italy. It is the most important grape variety in central Italy, especially in Tuscany. In this region, the surprisingly sophisticated Etruscans made delicious wine well before the rise of the Roman Empire. The Sangiovese grape tends to generate closely related mutations. In fact, the Brunello and Sangioveto grapes are such close relatives of Sangiovese that they are usually considered to be Sangiovese itself.

It might be said that, in terms of style, Sangiovese is to Nebbiolo what Pinot Noir is to Cabernet Sauvignon. Like an excellent Burgundy, many great Sangiovese wines, while age-worthy, can also be quite enjoyable before their fifth birthday.

Suggested Food Pairings

Because of its combination of characteristics, Sangiovese has few equals as a red wine to accompany seafood. When matching food and wine, remember also to match price along with other characteristics. In this sense, inexpensive, varietally labeled Sangiovese is a good pizza and spaghetti wine. These wines are usually better than those inexpensive, silly-looking, straw-covered bottles of cheap Chianti you used to see at Italian restaurants. The "super-Tuscan" red wines that first came to our market in the early 1980s are a blend of Sangiovese and Cabernet Sauvignon. These superior wines lie outside of Italy's wine classification system, but they are more intensely flavored than Chianti and are worth a try if you are looking to splurge.

Like other noble grape varieties, Sangiovese can be a prince or a pauper, and the pauper, a varietal-labeled Sangiovese from one of Italy's many regions, is frequently a bargain. Early attempts at this varietal in California tend to cost like the prince but taste like the pauper. So far, California winemakers have had a difficult time getting Sangiovese acclimated to the warmth and sunshine of their vineyards. However, a few producers have produced some good Sangioveses, albeit at Sauvignon-like prices.

Varietally labeled Sangiovese can be surprisingly inexpensive. Look for the typical cherry fruit, high acid, low tannin, and glycerine.

In the Chianti region, the Sangiovese grape has historically been blended with the local Canaiolo grape as well as two white grapes: Trebbiano and Malvasia. Presently, the top producers are omitting the white grapes, in favor of more Sangiovese.

Recommended Sangiovese

Name	Region	Price
Gini, Chianti DOCG *straw bottle*	Tuscany, Italy	$
La Carraia, Sangiovese IGT	Umbria, Italy	$
Poliziano, Rosso di Montepulciano 2002	Tuscany, Italy	$
Fattoria Le Pupille, Morellino di Scansano 2002	Tuscany, Italy	$
Long Vineyards "Seghesio Vineyards"	Sonoma, CA	$$
Poliziano, Vino Nobile di Montepulciano 2000	Tuscany, Italy	$$
Altesino, Rosso di Montalcino 2002	Tuscany, Italy	$$
Altesino, Brunello di Montalcino 1998	Tuscany, Italy	$$$
Antinori "Tignanello" 2000	Tuscany, Italy	$$$
Castello di Ama, Chianti Classico DOCG "Casuccia" 1997	Tuscany, Italy	$$$$

Grenache

Main growing regions: Spain, Rhône (France), and California
Aromas and flavors: Raspberry
Tannin: Low
Acidity: Moderate
Body: Medium to full
Major mixing partners: Syrah (France) and Tempranillo (Spain)

The Southern Rhône Valley of France is famous for its sturdy, drinkable, and affordable red wines. Many different grape varieties are grown here, but Grenache is the predominant variety and is the primary grape among the many used to make Côtes du Rhône Rouge. This popular wine has ample body, meaty structure, and a straightforward fruit flavor of raspberry jam. Côtes du Rhône is a genuine bargain among French red wines, usually retailing for less than $10 per bottle. The dry rosés of the neighboring Southern French regions are also made primarily from the Grenache grape and are considered by many experts to be the finest pink wines in the world.

Suggested Food Pairings

Well-made Grenache-based wines tend to have enough body and character to be enjoyable with or without food. Hearty beef and lamb dishes, especially stews made with Côtes-du-Rhône as an ingredient, seem to bring out the delightful spiciness in Grenache. The most powerful versions of Châteauneuf-du-Pape stand up well to steak au poivre and other powerfully seasoned dishes, whereas tamer bottlings match well with goose, duck, and the like—not summer food, and not summer wine. In hot weather, try pairing a French Tavel or a California rosé with a salad or simple picnic fare.

Under the local name Garnacha, Grenache is extensively planted in Spain and Portugal. It lends some fruit to the relatively austere Tempranillo grape in the red wines of Rioja (Spain). In California, it is vinified in bulk for use in rosés and red jug wines, although some wineries are experimenting with upscale rosés.

To experience Grenache in its purest state, look for Château Rayas from Châteauneuf-du-Pape. Although AOC law allows the use of as many as thirteen different grapes for Châteauneuf-du-Pape red, most of these wines are predominantly Grenache, and Château Rayas eschews all other permitted varieties to make a 100-percent Grenache wine. This costs more than $100 per bottle, though.

Recommended Grenache/Garnacha

Name	Region	Price
Principe de Viana, Agramont "Old Vine" Garnacha	Navarra, Spain	$
Guigal Côtes du Rhône	Rhône, France	$
Bonny Doon "Clos de Gilroy"	California	$
Domaine Montirius Gigondas	Rhône, France	$$
Domaine de La Janasse Châteauneuf-du-Pape	Rhône, France	$$
Alban "Estate Vineyard"	Edna Valley, CA	$$$

Gamay

Main growing region: Beaujolais (France)
Aromas and flavors: Strawberries and raspberries
Acidity: Moderate
Tannin: Low
Body: Light
Major mixing partners: None

The granite soil of the Beaujolais, the southernmost sub-region of Burgundy, brings out the best qualities of the Gamay grape. The red wine of Beaujolais is fresh, light, and fruity, and it is enjoyed all over the world. The lively fruit flavors—strawberry and raspberry—show well in the absence of substantial tannin. These qualities lend themselves well to carbonic maceration (whole berry fermentation in the complete absence of oxygen). This process protects the delicate fruit components and readies the wine for early release.

Beaujolais Nouveau, the first release of red Beaujolais, reaches the market the third Thursday in November, immediately following the harvest. It is eagerly awaited by the wine world as the first indication of the quality of the entire vintage, so a delicious Beaujolais Nouveau is cause for rejoicing among the French.

The Gamay grape reaches its summit of quality in the "cru Beaujolais" wines. These are red wines produced from Gamay grapes grown within the ten townships regarded as superior to the rest of the subregion: Moulin-à-Vent, Brouilly, Côte de Brouilly, Fleurie, Chiroubles, Morgon, Chénas, Juliénas, Saint-Amour, and Régnié. Taken together, these townships comprise the heart of the Beaujolais subregion. It has been observed that these wines, unlike other wines from Beaujolais, can benefit from a few years of aging.

Suggested Food Pairings

With its pleasant balance of fruit over tannin, a Gamay-based wine can take a slight chilling and may be offered with just about any food, from poached salmon to barbecued pork ribs. These wines, with their overt fruitiness, are also enjoyable alone.

California does produce, albeit sparingly, two wines whose names imply Gamay—Napa Gamay and Gamay Beaujolais. Napa Gamay is actually the lowly Gros Auxerrois grape from Southwest France, and Gamay Beaujolais is an inferior mutation of Pinot Noir. For price and quality, stick to the French version, especially during the Nouveau season when California "Gamay Nouveau" labels are intentionally deceiving and the wines are decidedly inferior to the real thing.

The Georges Duboeuf firm is the king of Beaujolais wine producers. The quality and pricing of its wines are more than fair. Louis Jadot is another reliable bottler of Beaujolais. These two firms bottle the full spectrum of wine from this subregion: Beaujolais Nouveau, Beaujolais-Villages, and all of the *crus*.

Recommended Gamay		
Name	Region	Price
Georges Duboeuf, Beaujolais-Villages	Beaujolais, Burgundy, France	$
Domaine des Braves, Régnié	Beaujolais, Burgundy, France	$
Louis Jadot, Moulin-à-Vent "Château des Jacques"	Beaujolais, Burgundy, France	$

Tempranillo

Main growing regions: Rioja (Spain)
Aromas and flavors: Not very fruity; leather, spice, cherries, and raisins
Acidity: Low to moderate
Tannin: Low to moderate
Body: Medium
Major mixing partner: Grenache/Garnacha (Rioja)

You rarely see Tempranillo bottled as a varietal, but it is included here because of the importance of Rioja, an affordable treasure from Spain. Tempranillo-based Rioja-region wines range from very inexpensive but enjoyable varieties to fabulously expensive, world-class versions. The inexpensive versions often display the body of Pinot Noir without the flashy fruit. The subtle cherry fruit of Tempranillo is often well masked by smoky flavors and oakiness. Grenache (Garnacha) is the minority blending partner in Rioja, and it adds some fruitiness to the wine. The greatest versions of Rioja cost as much as any great wine and show a depth and length of flavors that justify their price.

The Tempranillo-based Rioja wines are a great value, and they are easy to appreciate. Rioja is a good place for the neophyte to start in his or her exploration of red wine.

Suggested Food Pairings

As a light- to medium-bodied red with modest acidity, red Rioja matches well with grilled fish, generously seasoned vegetable dishes, and pasta. It also pairs well with chicken and red meats. As such, Rioja might accurately be called a fool-proof red wine.

Recommended Tempranillo/Tinto Fino		
Name	**Region**	**Price**
Bodegas Bretón "Loriñón" Tinto	Rioja Alta	$
Clos du Bois	Alexander Valley, Sonoma, CA	$
Bodegas Montecillo, Rioja Gran Reserva	Rioja	$$
Teófilo Reyes	Ribero del Duero	$$
Truchard	Napa Valley, CA	$$
Pesquera Reserva	Ribero del Duero	$$$

Malbec

Main growing regions: Bordeaux and Cahors (France), Argentina
Aromas and flavors: Raspberry, chocolate, and spice
Acidity: Can be low or moderately high depending on origin
Tannin: High
Body: Medium to full
Major mixing partners: Other Bordeaux varieties

Malbec ripens early, usually a week or so after the Merlot is harvested. Malbec is a relatively minor Bordeaux variety, but it has managed to attain stardom on its own. Malbec is often the primary grape variety in the Côtes de Blaye sub-region of Bordeaux, which is situated across the Gironde River from the Médoc. Although it is used less and less in Bordeaux, Malbec is the main grape in the wines of Cahors, in Southwestern France. Malbec has not caught on especially well in California, where it is used sparingly in "Meritage" wines.

Argentina, however, is another story. A century ago, the Malbec grape was brought to Argentina, where it thrives in the hot, dry summers of the eastern foothills of the Andes. Malbec may well be considered the national grape of Argentina, and there are many quality versions on the market for less than $10. Argentinean producers have been focusing more and more on quality in the past decade, and some increasingly pricey—and exquisite—Argentine Malbecs have been reaching our shelves and scoring well with the wine critics. Don't be too shocked to see $50 versions in your wine shop . . . dollar for dollar, these Malbecs compete favorably with Californian Cabernet Sauvignons.

Suggested Food Pairings

The Argentines enjoy their Malbecs with their famously grass-fed beef. The growing movement toward naturally raised, grass-fed beef provides us with an easy match with full-bodied Argentine Malbec.

Recommended Malbec		
Name	**Region**	**Price**
Gascón	Argentina	$
Château du Cèdre 2000	Cahors, France	$
Ricardo Santos	Argentina	$
Château Roland La Garde 2000	Côtes de Blaye, Bordeaux	$$
Catena "Alta"	Argentina	$$$

Cabernet Franc

Main growing regions: Bordeaux and Loire (France), California, and Northeastern U.S.
Aromas and flavors: Cherries, pencil lead, dust, currants, and herbs
Acidity: Moderate
Tannin: Moderate to low
Body: Light
Major mixing partners: Other Bordeaux varieties

Cabernet Franc, "the other Cabernet," in Bordeaux, is more commonly used in blends than as a standalone varietal wine. Recent DNA analysis suggests that Cabernet Franc is a parent grape of Cabernet Sauvignon. Although

Cabernet Franc grapes require ample heat accumulation in order to ripen fully, the Cabernet Franc vine is perhaps the hardiest of all *vinifera* vines and is able to withstand a harshly cold winter. For this reason alone there is considerable acreage of Cabernet Franc growing in the northeastern United States. However, it appears that few northeastern vineyards other than those on the especially warm North Fork of Long Island can bring this grape to full ripeness.

There are several excellent Californian versions of Cabernet Franc, although they are overshadowed by the more popular Cabernet Sauvignons. Cabernet Franc is a star in France's Loire Valley, where it is made into a light and agreeable red in the appellations Chinon and Bourgueil. In Bordeaux, the earlier-ripening Cabernet Franc offers a safety net to Médoc *vignerons* whose later-ripening Cabernet Sauvignon may be damaged by autumn rains. Across the Dordogne River, Cabernet Franc is an important blending partner to Merlot in the Saint-Émilion district.

Recommended Cabernet Franc

Name	Region	Price
Ironstone	California	$
Domaine Charles Joguet Chinon	Loire Valley, France	$
Standing Stone	Finger Lakes, NY	$
Pride Mountain Vineyards	Sonoma, CA	$$$
Château Cheval Blanc 1998	Saint-Émilion, Bordeaux	$$$$

Barbera

Main growing regions: Piedmont, Lombardy (Italy), the Central Valley of California
Aromas and flavors: Indistinct aromas, strong "grapey" flavors
Acidity: Moderate to rapier-like
Tannin: Light
Body: Medium
Major mixing partners: Barbera sneaks into some Nebbiolo-based Piedmont wines; also blended with Zinfandel for "jug" wine in California

While the Nebbiolo is Piedmont's royal grape, Barbera is perhaps the region's most useful. Ripening after the Dolcetto but before the Nebbiolo, Barbera makes a hearty, powerful wine whose prominent acidity makes it compatible with assertively flavored Piedmontese dishes. In California, the Barbera grape is relegated to workhorse status. Like the white Chenin Blanc, Barbera maintains its high acidity at high crop levels and in the blistering heat of California's vast San Joaquin Valley.

Recommended Barbera		
Name	Region	Price
Martilde, Barbera Oltrepò Pavese DOC	Lombardy, Italy	$
Cantina del Pino, Barbera d'Alba DOC	Piedmont, Italy	$
Coppo "Camp du Rouss" Barbera d'Asti DOC	Piedmont, Italy	$
Renwood	Amador, CA	$$

White Wine Grapes

Chardonnay

Main growing regions: Burgundy (France), California, Oregon, Washington State, Australia, New Zealand, South Africa, and Chile
Aromas and flavors: Varies greatly by region: vanilla, tropical fruits, toast, and nuts
Acidity: Moderate to high
Body: Light to moderate
Major mixing partners: Sémillon (Australia)

The wine-drinking public is so accustomed to saying, "I'll have a Chardonnay," it's worth reminding that Chardonnay is the name of a white-wine grape variety. In fact, Chardonnay is the most popular and most versatile white grape in the world, though it is not the most widely planted one. (That distinction belongs to Spain's Airén grape.) Chardonnay grapes are used to make the austere, bone-dry wines of France's Chablis subregion, as well as the tropically fruity, almost syrupy white wines of California and Australia. It is also a crucial component of Champagne and the sole grape in the premium Champagne labeled "Blanc de Blancs." Chardonnay is responsible for the great white Burgundies from France—the most expensive dry white wines in the world. Finally, Chardonnay can even accommodate a dose of noble rot and yield a gloriously rich and sweet dessert wine, as it does in Southeastern Austria and elsewhere.

What makes Chardonnay so versatile? Perhaps Chardonnay has little indigenous character of its own and instead displays the best characteristics of the soil and climate in which it is grown, like a lawyer who can argue any side of an issue. However, in all of its incarnations, Chardonnay does display a propensity for both glycerine and acid, whose interplay results in the most velvety, sensually delightful texture of all white wines. So, under all its trappings, Chardonnay is mostly about texture, and that is what you should always look for, even in simple Chardonnays. Unlike the red-wine kingpin Cabernet Sauvignon, there are many high-quality Chardonnays to be found in the $8 to $10 price range.

So what does Chardonnay taste like? It depends on whom you ask. It is difficult to define a standard of varietal correctness when a grape variety has so many personalities. However, some generalizations about Chardonnay can be made.

The astringent flavor imparted by oak barrels marries well with Chardonnay in different regions. So well, in fact, that it can be difficult to separate the flavor of the grape and the flavor of the oak in your mind. If you want to taste a pure, unoaked Chardonnay, look for a Chablis from the producer Jean-Marc Brocard, another of the handful of Chablis producers who eschew the use of oak in their winemaking.

To the south of Chablis in France is the Burgundy subregion of Côte de Beaune, where Chardonnay grapes are transformed into the world's greatest Chardonnay wines. Corton-Charlemagne, Meursault, and the various Montrachet vineyards produce beautifully structured Chardonnays that are brilliant and clean, with acidity, mouth-filling body, and aromas of toast, nuts, butter, and a variety of subtle fruits. When ripened in the California sunshine, the fruit aroma becomes more apparent.

Suggested Food Pairings

Because Chardonnay has such a range of styles, you should consider the type of Chardonnay when trying to find the right wine for a particular meal. Chablis is the driest, most acidic interpretation, and belongs with seafood, especially shellfish and delicate white fish like Dover sole or wild halibut. The rounder white Burgundies from the Côte de Beaune are also seafood wines but can accompany meats such as chicken and veal. However, seafood doesn't match so well with fruitier Chardonnays such as those from California and Australia.

If you insist on a fruity Chardonnay with your fish, California cuisine comes into play. The flavorful ingredients used in California cuisine— generous additions of fresh herbs and various chili peppers, and wood grilling—can transform a delicate piece of fish into a jam session of loud flavors. In this case, a big wine is called for, and California Chardonnay is ideal. In fact, big Chardonnays like these can stand up to many dishes not normally paired with white wine—even grilled meats! Finally, if you want to drink Chardonnay without food, the Australian versions, with their generous fruit and mild acidity, are an excellent choice.

Napa Valley, the first California appellation to excel with Chardonnay, tends to produce high-glycerine, well-oaked versions with ample fruit—apple and pear intermingled with oak. Drive over the Mayacamas mountain range into Sonoma Valley and you will find a more tropical element in Chardonnay, usually pineapple. The Santa Barbara growing area, far south of Napa/Sonoma, tends to bottle an even riper

Chardonnay. The fruit impression there is even more tropical, and the acidity profile is quite soft.

For yet more fruit flavor, you must go to Australia. The grape-growing climate in Australia is unique to wine-producing countries. The Hunter Valley in Southeastern Australia experiences intense sunshine. This would normally overripen wine grapes, but the ripening effect of the sun in this region is greatly tempered by cool breezes. This combination of plentiful sunlight and refreshing air brings grapes to a full ripeness slowly, so as to develop the most intense flavors imaginable in Chardonnay. Suggestions of pineapple, coconut, and bananas spring forth from this deep-golden wine. These wines used to lack the necessary acidity, but innovative winemaking techniques seem to have solved this problem.

Recommended Chardonnay

Name	Region	Price
Lindeman's Bin 65	Padthaway, Australia	$
Maison Louis Latour "Grand Ardèche" l'Ardèche	Vin de Pays des Coteaux	$
Château St. Jean	Sonoma, CA	$
Brocard Chablis "Domaine Sainte Claire"	Chablis, Burgundy, France	$
Hamilton Russell Vineyards "Estate"	Walker Bay, South Africa	$$
Kumeu River 2002	Kumeu, North Island, New Zealand	$$
Château Ste. Michelle "Cold Creek Vineyard"	Columbia Valley, WA	$$
Long Vineyards "Estate Grown"	Napa Valley, CA	$$
Leeuwin Estate "Art Series"	Margret River, Australia	$$$
Domaine Louis Latour Corton-Charlemagne 2001	Burgundy, France	$$$

Sauvignon Blanc

Main growing regions: Bordeaux (France), Loire (France), California, New Zealand, and South Africa
Aromas and flavors: Cut grass, herbs, melon, gooseberry, and grapefruit; cat-box, in extreme versions
Acidity: High
Body: Light to medium
Major mixing partner: Sémillon (Bordeaux)

In comparison to Chardonnay, it might take a little more wine knowledge to appreciate a great Sauvignon Blanc. That is because the hallmark of quality Sauvignon Blanc—bright, crisp acidity—is not as sensually pleasing as the seductive texture of good Chardonnay. "Grassy " and "herbaceous" are common descriptions of Sauvignon Blanc's fruit components.

An alternative vinification style of Sauvignon Blanc yields a richer wine. "Fumé Blanc" is the name for a style created in California in the 1960s by Robert Mondavi. Styled after the legendary Pouilly-Fumé of the Loire region in France, Fumé Blanc has a richer, fuller style.

There are a few world-class wines made from Sauvignon Blanc that earn this variety its place beside the other white noble grapes, Riesling and Chardonnay. Château Haut-Brion Blanc of Graves is universally regarded as the finest of its type and an equal to the great white Burgundies. Close on its heels is Domaine de Chevalier, also from Graves. Sauvignon Blanc is blended with a lesser amount of Sémillon in most Graves whites. This formula is reversed in the dessert wines from neighboring Sauternes.

In spite of its legitimate claim to nobility, Sauvignon Blanc might well have an inferiority complex. The public hasn't taken to this variety like it has to Chardonnay. Some winemakers have even employed a heavy-handed oaking to make Sauvignon Blanc seem more like Chardonnay. Fortunately, low demand has kept the prices down somewhat.

Suggested Food Pairings

The high acidity of Sauvignon Blanc makes for a great pairing with seafood—Sancerre from the Loire; Graves Blanc from Bordeaux; and varietal Sauvignon Blanc from California, South Africa, and even New Zealand are perfect with fish. Whereas the Sauvignon Blancs are excellent with seafood, the more substantial Fumé Blanc can be paired with a wider variety of dishes, including chicken, veal, and pasta. Try serving a good Sauvignon Blanc with an uncomplicated seafood dish without telling your guests what they are drinking, and you will seem quite wine savvy once they figure it out.

Recommended Sauvignon Blanc

Name	Region	Price
Kim Crawford Sauvignon Blanc	Marlborough, New Zealand	$
Matanzas Creek Sauvignon Blanc, 2012	Sonoma, CA	$
Grgich Hills Fumé Blanc	Napa Valley, CA	$$
Château La Louvière Blanc Pessac, 2012	Pessac, Bourdeaux, France	$$$

Riesling

Main growing regions: Germany, Austria, Alsace (France), Washington, New York's Finger Lakes district, and California
Aromas and flavors: Apricots, citrus, peaches, and flowers
Acidity: Moderate to high

Body: Light; medium to heavy for dessert wines
Major mixing partners: None (Riesling is often blended with lesser varieties in nonvarietal German QbA wines.)

Just as Pinot Noir rivals Cabernet Sauvignon for preeminence among noble red varieties, the Riesling grape has a following that regards it as superior to Chardonnay. Like Pinot Noir, Riesling has not traveled as well as its rival. Both Pinot Noir and Riesling turn shy in the warmth of California and require a cooler climate in order to perform well. Whereas the demand for quality Pinot Noir has motivated American winemakers to seek out promising vineyards for growing it, Riesling has never been in high demand in the United States.

Suggested Food Pairings

Drier versions are good with seafood, particularly shellfish. Riesling served with lobster is a very good match.

Perhaps if Riesling had been widely planted in France it would have found its niche in French gastronomy and secured its immortality. However, Riesling is only permitted to grow in French soil in the Alsace region of France.

In general, the aroma of well-made Riesling is flowery as well as fruity, and Riesling smells sweeter than Chardonnay. In fact, Riesling's alleged sweetness has kept it out of the fast lane in today's wine market. While it is true that Riesling grapes can make sweet wine—their prominent acidity provides the perfect balance for late-harvest sweetness, and they can produce the sweetest dessert wines in the world—

some other excellent Rieslings, notably those from Alsace and Austria, can be nearly bone dry.

Riesling has long been the basis for the finest wines of Germany. The steep slopes along the Rhine and Mosel rivers retain warmth and incubate the Riesling to full ripeness in the otherwise chilly climate. Attaining the sweetness needed to become a good dessert wine in such a northerly climate is quite a victory over nature.

Although the Sémillon-based dessert wines from Sauternes, France, are equally noteworthy as world-class dessert wines, these wines need some acidic Sauvignon Blanc blended in to balance the flaccid sweetness of *botrytis*-affected Sémillon. Sweet Riesling need not be blended.

Some of the best values in the wine world today are the German Rieslings designated QbA (*Qualitätswein bestimmter Anbaugebiete*, or "quality wine") and labeled "Riesling." The superior QmP (*Qualitätswein mit Prädikat*, or "highest quality") white wines from Germany are, by definition, made from Riesling unless labeled otherwise.

There have been some notable successes with Riesling in North America, many outside of California. Oregon, Washington State, Idaho, New York State, and Canada all produce quality Rieslings.

Be wary of imitations! Several lowly grape varieties, including Gray Riesling and Welschriesling, are deceptively named and have nothing to do with the real thing. Look for wines labeled "Riesling," "White Riesling," or "Johannisberg Riesling." Don't be afraid of an older bottle. Rieslings have demonstrated a capacity to improve with age, much more so than Chardonnays. This is especially true of the Alsace and German Rieslings.

Recommended Riesling

Name	Region	Price
St.Urbans-Hof QbA	Mosel-Saar-Ruwer, Germany	$
Dr. Konstantin Frank "Semi-Dry"	Finger Lakes, NY	$
Kurt Darting Dürkheimer Michelsberg Kabinett 2002	Pfalz, Germany	$
Joh. Haart, Piesporter Goldtröpfchen Kabinett 2002	Mosel, Germany	$
Château Ste. Michelle-Dr. Loosen "Eroica"	Washington State	$
Schloss Johannisberger QbA 2002	Rheingau, Germany	$$
Nikolaihof "Federspiel"	Wachau, Austria	$$
Domaine Weinbach "Réserve Personnelle"	Alsace, France	$$
Joh. Jos. Prüm, Wehlener Sonnenuhr Spätlese 2002	Mosel, Germany	$$
Grosset "Polish Hill"	Clare Valley, Australia	$$

Chenin Blanc

Main growing regions: Loire (France), South Africa, New Zealand, and California
Aromas and flavors: Somewhat muted; melon, honey
Acidity: Often very high
Body: Light to medium
Major mixing partners: Sometimes blended with Chardonnay in the Loire region

Chenin Blanc is widely grown around the world and has several distinct personalities. In the Loire Valley of Northwestern France, where it has been cultivated for over a thousand years, Chenin Blanc is responsible for the acidic white wines of Anjou and Touraine. The best known of these is Vouvray, which itself can take several forms.

Vouvray, whose name comes from the village in Touraine where it is produced, is the most weather-sensitive table wine. Whereas winemakers elsewhere usually attempt to produce a consistent style from vintage to vintage, Vouvray is made in different styles depending on the weather. A pleasant, sunny summer brings the Chenin Blanc grapes in Vouvray to full ripeness. In such years, demi-sec (half-dry) wine is produced. A cold and rainy summer is unwelcome in any vineyard. Rather than gnash their teeth, though, winemakers respond by making Vouvray sec. This dry version of Chenin Blanc is very acidic. Vouvray sec has a following among connoisseurs who prize naked acidity. On the other end of the sweetness spectrum is Quarts de Chaume, a melony, honeyed dessert wine made from *botrytis*-affected Chenin Blanc from Anjou in the Loire Valley. These sweet wines are said to live indefinitely in the bottle, as do the sweeter versions of the Vouvray demi-sec.

High acidity is the backbone of well-made sparkling wine, and the naturally acidic Chenin Blanc grape is used to make high-quality sparkling wine in the Loire region. Semisparkling wine labeled "Vouvray Mousseux" is common, and the great Champagne firm of Taittinger produces its Bouvet Brut from Chenin Blanc in the Loire. These sparkling wines, though not as complex as true Champagne, are often made just as well and offer excellent value.

Chenin Blanc has traveled abroad with success. It was brought to South Africa in the 1600s by Dutch settlers and is widely grown there under the name of Steen. In California, Chenin Blanc is extensively cultivated for use in brandy-making and as part of the mix in jug wines. Chenin Blanc is capable of retaining its acidity at high yields and in high temperatures, a quality that makes it an economically important variety for high-volume production.

There have also been many pleasant and enjoyable California Chenin Blancs sold as varietal wines, but their popularity is fading. The best of these display the same honey and melon aromas as Quarts de Chaume with moderate acidity—perfect summer wines. In addition to its use in California jug wines, Chenin Blanc is sometimes blended with Chardonnay in New Zealand and in Loire.

Suggested Food Pairings

In general, Chenin Blanc–based wines match well with summer foods. Because of their high acidity, restrained fruit, and balance, well-made versions can be a welcome respite from your usual white wine. These wines have a natural affinity with sweet shellfish like sea scallops, but are also enjoyable with anything light, such as pasta, fish, and chicken.

Demi-sec wines have a pleasant level of residual sugar, but they are dry enough to enjoy with dinner. Chenin Blanc's inherent bracing acidity provides ample balance to the sweetness in demi-sec wines. These wines match well with a wide variety of light dishes. Vouvray sec is difficult to enjoy without food and is best matched with fresh shellfish.

Recommended Chenin Blanc		
Name	**Region**	**Price**
Marc Brédif Vouvray	Loire Valley, France	$
Chappellet "Old Vine Cuvée"	Napa Valley, CA	$
Mulderbosch	Stellenbosch, South Africa	$
S.A. Huët "Le Haut-Lieu" Vouvray Demi-Sec	Loire Valley, France	$$
Domaine des Baumard Quarts de Chaume 2000 (375ml)	Loire Valley, France	$$

The Book of Wine

Pinot Blanc

Main growing regions: Burgundy (France), Alsace (France), Italy, Austria, and California
Aromas and flavors: Somewhat subdued, almonds and apples
Acidity: Moderate to high
Body: Medium to full
Major mixing partners: Rarely blended; formerly with Chardonnay in Burgundy

Also known as Pinot Bianco in Italy, Pinot Blanc is recognized for its simple, full-bodied, clean structure and forward acidity. It is used (in combination with other grapes) for some premium sparkling wines in California. Not widely produced in California, Pinot Blanc can be a good value among Alsace wines.

Originally grown in ancient Burgundy, Pinot Blanc has long been cultivated side by side with Chardonnay. Indeed, some mutations of Pinot Blanc are capable of producing a Chardonnay-like wine. But for the most part, Pinot Blanc makes a rather nondescript wine with weak aroma. More than any other grape variety, Pinot Blanc can make a perfect "background wine," one that knows how to let elaborately flavored foods be the star of the dinner.

Suggested Food Pairings

Because it usually makes an uncomplicated wine, Pinot Blanc is enjoyable with a wide variety of dishes and doesn't require careful matching. Although Pinot Blanc is typically good with food, it can often be quite boring without.

Name	Region	Price
Alois Lageder Pinot Bianco	Trentino-Alto Adige, Italy	$
Polz Weissburgunder	Südsteiermark, Austria	$
Colterenzio Pinot Bianco "Weisshaus"	Trentino-Aldo Adige, Italy	$
Paul Blanck "Pinot Blanc d'Alsace"	Alsace, France	$
Steele	Santa Barbara, CA	$

Sémillon

Main growing regions: Bordeaux (France), Australia, and California
Aromas and flavors: Figs, honey, and lemon
Acidity: Low to medium
Body: Full
Major mixing partners: Sauvignon Blanc (Bordeaux)

The Sémillon grape rarely stands alone as a varietal. It is often blended in the Graves subregion of Bordeaux, France, with Sauvignon Blanc. Its silky richness is offset perfectly by the complementary acidity of Sauvignon Blanc. Sémillon is the main variety in Sauternes, the dessert wine–producing subregion of Bordeaux. These wines also have Sauvignon Blanc mixed in to give them a little acidity. Good and affordable dessert Sémillon, in its pure form, is produced in Australia.

Its signature characteristics are low acidity and thick body, and its aromas and flavors of figs, honey, and lemon are restrained. This set of qualities does not add up to an exceptional table wine, although good, inexpensive varietal Sémillon is available. However, Sémillon's propensity for richness and its susceptibility to "noble rot" make it a useful grape variety, albeit one with limited applications.

Recommended Sémillon		
Name	Region	Price
Australian Peter Lehmann Botrytis Sémillon (375ml)	Barossa Valley, Australia	$
Beringer "Alluvium" White	Knights Valley, Sonoma, CA	$
Brokenwood	Lower Hunter Valley, Australia	$
L'Ecole No. 41 "Seven Hills Estate"	Walla Walla Valley, WA	$$

Viognier

Main growing regions: Rhône (France) and California
Aromas and flavors: Apricots, wood, peaches, and flowers
Acidity: Low to medium
Body: Medium to full
Major mixing partners: None

The long-unheralded Viognier grape has been producing some fine alternatives to Chardonnay in France's upper Rhône. Viognier's popularity is fairly recent as a varietal from California. Its apricot/peach flavors are a refreshing alternative to the perhaps repetitive pear/vanilla flavors of California Chardonnay. In fact, Viognier's biggest asset may be its vastly different flavor structure compared to Chardonnay, making it a good choice for those seeking an alternative to the latter.

The Northern Rhône Valley of Condrieu is Viognier's home turf. The smallest recognized appellation in France is Château-Grillet, a single estate within Condrieu. The

Viognier grape approaches world-class status at this tiny property: A bottle of Château-Grillet fetches $100 or more, and it is said to age well forever in the bottle. Less expensive but certainly noteworthy versions of Viognier come from the surrounding Condrieu vineyards.

California Viognier is not any cheaper than Chardonnay. For bargains, look for varietal Viognier from big French producers. Inexpensive *Vin de Pays* varietal Viognier has caught on in the French countryside, at least for export. These wines are often good values in terms of quality when compared with similarly priced Chardonnay.

Suggested Food Pairings

At its best, Viognier has aromas and flavors of peach, apricot, and flowers, though it is not as overtly flowery as Riesling. With the aromas and flavors of these particular fruits, Viognier is a natural match with pork, which has an affinity for both. However, if you substitute Viognier for Chardonnay in any food-wine pairing, you won't be disappointed.

Recommended Viognier		
Name	**Region**	**Price**
Château Pesquié	Côtes du Ventoux, Rhône, France	$
Zaca Mesa	Santa Ynez, CA	$
Alban	Central Coast, CA	$
Jaffurs	Santa Barbara, CA	$$
Guigal Condrieu	Rhone, France	$$$

Pinot Grigio/Pinot Gris

Main growing regions: Italy, Alsace, Oregon, and California
Aromas and flavors: Somewhat muted; minerals, pine, and orange rind
Acidity: Medium (generally higher in Europe)
Body: Medium (generally heavier in the United States)
Major mixing partners: None

A close relative of Pinot Blanc, Pinot Grigio has recently become a very popular varietal wine from Italy. In Friuli and Alto Adige, two Northern regions of Italy, Pinot Grigio can produce a well-structured and acidic match for seafood, with somewhat muddled aromas. In warmer climates, however, the acidity level can be undesirably low. Pinot Grigio is a relatively recent visitor to California, where it has yet to succeed in making wines comparable to those in Northern Italy.

Alsatian soil brings out the best in several white varieties, and Pinot Grigio, known there as Tokay Pinot Gris, is one of them. This pink-skinned variety is not strong-willed and is a perfect vehicle for the Alsace *terroir*—rich, minerally soil flavors mingle with the acidity.

The Oregonians call their version Pinot Gris. The cool Willamette Valley appears to be a Pinot Gris–friendly growing region. These wines have stronger-than-usual Pinot Gris flavor, rich body, and the signature citrus aromas of Pinot Grigio. These wines tend to be more expensive than the Italian versions.

Recommended Pinot Gris/Pinot Grigio

Name	Region	Price
Pighin, Grave del Friuli	Friuli, Italy	$
Willamette Valley Vineyards	Oregon	$
Trimbach Reserve	Alsace, France	$
King Estate "Reserve"	Oregon	$
Maso Poli	Trentino-Alto Adige, Italy	$
Jermann	Friuli, Italy	$$
Domaine Zind-Humbrecht "Clos Windsbuhl"	Alsace, France	$$$

Suggested Food Pairings

Because it doesn't have prominent fruit flavors, Pinot Grigio is relatively easy to match with food. The drier, more acidic versions are excellent with shellfish and other seafoods, whereas the fuller-bodied versions can accompany chicken and pasta dishes well.

Gewürztraminer

Main growing regions: Germany, Alsace (France), and California

Aromas and flavors: Strong lychee-nut fruit, rose petal, and grapefruit rind

Acidity: Low to medium

Body: Full

Major mixing partners: None

Gewürztraminer (pronounced gah-VERTS-truh-MEEN-er) is a pink-skinned clone of the much older Traminer vine that probably originated in Northern Italy. "Gewürz-" is German for "spicy" or "pungent" and reflects the powerful aromas of Gewürztraminer wines. It is the least subtle of all the well-known *vinifera* grapes. Although it grows best in Alsace (France), it plays second fiddle there to the Riesling grape. Its share of vineyard space in Germany has been on the decline, again being outmuscled by the Riesling grape. California and Pacific Northwest versions of this quirky variety tend to lack the complexity of their European counterparts, but can be both enjoyable and affordable.

Recommended Gewürztraminer

Name	Region	Price
Standing Stone	Finger Lakes, NY	$
Martinelli	Russian River Valley, Sonoma, CA	$
Navarro	Mendocino, CA	$$
Domaine Zind-Humbrecht "Turckheim"	Alsace, France	$$
Domaine Weinbach "Cuvée Ste. Catherine"	Alsace, France	$$$

Suggested Food Pairings

Rich, pungent, spicy flavors with fruit notes of lychee and grapefruit rind make for a difficult food-wine pairing. As such, Gewürztraminer is often suggested with spicy Asian food—an awkward blind date at best. Regional tradition in Alsace matches Gewürztraminer with sausage and ham. Because of its low acidity and bold flavors, Gewürztraminer can be enjoyable without food. Alternatively, a simple, creamy cheese provides a good background for the complex, full personality of this grape.

Grüner Veltliner

Major growing areas: Eastern Austria
Aromas and Flavors: Green beans, lentils, and ground pepper
Acidity: Moderate
Body: Medium to full
Major mixing partners: None

This once obscure grape variety has risen to prominence in the last decade for two reasons—the wines of Austria are usually very well made, and Grüner Veltliner is quite food-friendly. One well-known wine importer described Grüner Veltliner as tasting like the offspring of Riesling and Sauvignon Blanc.

Recommended Grüner Veltliner		
Name	**Region**	**Price**
Glatzer	Carnuntum, Austria	$
Familie Nigl "Kremser Freiheit"	Kremstal, Austria	$
R&A Pfaffl "Goldjoch"	Weinviertel, Austria	$
Bründlmayer "Alte Reben"	Kamptal, Austria	$$
Nikolaihof Smaragd Trocken	Wachau, Austria	$$$

Suggested Food Pairings

Grüner Veltliner has caught on recently among wine stewards and their more savvy clientele because it is compatible with so many dishes—even well-known wine-killers such as asparagus and artichokes. Grüner Veltliner often shows up on wine lists in upscale Asian restaurants, particularly Vietnamese, where it is nicely paired with dishes seasoned with lemongrass and the other powerful and pungent seasonings characteristic of that cuisine.

CHAPTER 5

Wine Regions

Three short decades ago, there was little to discuss about wine regions outside of France, other than the Napa Valley, perhaps, where some brash young upstarts had demonstrated California's potential. What about German wine? A long and proud tradition to be sure, but too *sweet*. (Not necessarily true, then or today.) And what to do with Italian wine? Drink it with spaghetti and stick a candle in the empty. (It is true that back in the 1970s, the Italian wine industry was still being dragged, kicking and screaming, into the twentieth century.) South American wine cost about $2 and just gave you a headache . . . it was only a slight improvement over Mexican tap water. Australian wine? Banana juice! (This country's early efforts had a lot more fruit than acidity.) And forget South African Wine—that country was politically embargoed right out of the wine boom until the 1990s. New Zealand wine wasn't happening yet. And as for Spanish wine, it was good for making sangria, maybe. (Some old-style Spanish reds were aged for a decade in oak casks, robbing them of any fruit whatsoever.)

The wine world has changed considerably in the past thirty years. Scientific progress led to the large-scale modernization of commercial winemaking, which then made it possible to update traditional wine regions and develop new and promising sites all over the globe. Adventurous wine lovers can now enjoy high-quality wines from some twenty different nations whose wares usually reflect in some way the old European wine traditions and styles while also imparting some unique twists of their own.

The Home of the Vine

The wine grape thrives in weather conditions that are neither too hot nor too cold. Too much heat rushes the grapes to ripeness without allowing for full flavor development and then scorches their skins brown. A lack of adequate heat is also detrimental; it prevents grapes from ripening sufficiently, and fine wine production thus becomes economically, if not physically, impossible. The wine grape prefers moderate warmth, spread over seven or more frost-free months. Winter must be cold enough to draw the vines into dormancy, yet not much colder than that; even the hardiest *vinifera* stock cannot withstand a brutal, subzero cold snap without significant physiological damage. And so the primary determinant of a wine region's viability is the range of its temperatures over the course of the year.

Climate Conditions

As previously noted in this book, the ancient Greeks maintained that the realm of the wine grape was limited to that of the fig and the olive—a warm climate, indeed, not too far from the Mediterranean Sea. When the Romans pushed this arbitrary boundary northward into continental Europe, they demonstrated that viticulture was not only possible, it was even preferable, in cooler European climates as far north as the evergreen oak could thrive.

The wine regions of the world are found generally between the 30th and 50th degrees parallel, with certain exceptions. Quality viticulture is possible closer to the equator, in mountainous regions where the high altitude approximates the cooler conditions farther from the equator. Extreme northerly (or southerly) viticulture may be possible as well, when specific weather conditions—such as the Northeast Atlantic Gulf Stream or the alpine *föhn* (the warm downhill wind)—bring late-season warmth to the vineyards. Thus the macroclimate—the wine region's long-term, general weather pattern—is a prerequisite for fine wine production.

Ideal Soil

The wine grape, like all plants, needs water, but prefers dry climates to dampness. Rainfall is welcome in the springtime, but not right before the harvest, when it can swell the grapes and dilute the wine. Soils that easily drain themselves of moisture are ideal, and the soils of the great wine regions in the world are usually known for their stone and mineral content rather than their richness. The vineyard "soil" of the Châteauneuf-du-Pape region, for instance, is made up mostly of saucer-shaped white stones—*galettes*—that reflect the sun's rays toward the vines by day and release their stored energy at night, thus bringing the vines to a level of ripeness unmatched elsewhere in France. It is a great anomaly of viticulture that the grape vine—unlike almost every other cash crop on the planet—grows best in soils nearly devoid of biological nutrients.

Within the macroclimates bathed with appropriate amounts of warmth and sunshine, there are smaller pockets of land blessed with ideal soils for grape cultivation and shielded, one way or another, from excessive rains. Sometimes a local geographic feature—such as a south-facing hillside that easily gathers sunshine, or a deep river valley that holds autumn warmth a little later into the season—can result in a certain piece of land producing wines of particular distinction. This is known as a microclimate.

And so we have the elements of a successful wine region: macroclimate, microclimate, and soil. Taken together, these are known to the French as *terroir*—the set of climatic and geological qualities unique to a particular piece of land. It is because of this notion of *terroir* that the French and other European wine producers have long considered a wine's geographic origin to be of foremost importance, more important even than grape variety.

Against this backdrop, let us go on a tour of the wine-producing regions of the world.

France

France is the mother lode of fine wine, perfectly situated as it is along the sun-drenched Mediterranean and the balmy Atlantic Gulf Stream, and sliced by long river valleys that channel warmth to her inland vines. Nature's unparalleled gifts notwithstanding, it was through arduous trial and error that the French learned how to make very good wine. This ability developed only after centuries of careful cultivation and meticulous record keeping, particularly by the Church.

Indeed, it is not farfetched to say that the French have defined quality wine for the rest of the world. The wineries of California, South America, and Australia all strive to produce wine that will compare favorably with French wines, as if those were the gold standard. These New-World regions, especially California, may have succeeded in producing beautiful wines that often exceed their French counterparts in sheer power, but they rarely match the French wines when it comes to finesse.

It is generally accepted among wine experts that France produces many "best-of " wine types:

- The *tête de cuvée* Champagnes from the top houses are the finest sparkling wines in the world. Alsace Gewürztraminer is the best version of this quirky wine.
- The Haut-Médoc subregion of Bordeaux produces, in its greatest years, the finest Cabernet Sauvignon–based wines in the world.
- Merlot best displays its qualities in the Bordeaux subregions of Saint-Émilion and Pomerol.
- The *Grand Cru* vineyards of the Côte de Beaune produce the finest Chardonnays on Earth.
- The most refined Sauvignon Blanc–based wines are produced in the upper Loire subregions of Sancerre and Pouilly-Fumé, and the Graves subregion of Bordeaux.
- Chenin Blanc is in its glory along the middle Loire River.
- Sauternes, from the town of the same name, is widely acclaimed as the world's finest dessert wine.
- The prototype for world-class Pinot Noir comes from the vineyards of Côte de Nuits in Burgundy.
- For a simple, acidic shellfish wine, Muscadet is unparalleled.

- Finally, the dry rosé wines of Provence are considered to be the best of their type.

Except for those varietal wines aimed directly at the American market, French wines are usually labeled by geographical region (e.g., Bordeaux) rather than grape variety. This reflects the French view that geographic origin—*terroir*—is of supreme importance in producing quality wines. Other than inexpensive, varietally labeled *Vin de Pays* (country wine), only the wines from the Alsace region are labeled by their grape variety.

In order to understand the degrees of specificity of French wine labeling, think of an archery target. The outer circle is all of France; the next-largest circle is a region of France such as Bordeaux; the next circle is in the district of, say, Médoc; within that is the commune name—Pauillac, for instance; finally, the bull's eye is the individual producer, a château or domaine. The better (and more expensive) the wine, the more specific the indicated source of the wine will be.

Just as French society is hierarchical—sometimes ridiculously so—so is her classification of her beloved wines. A general understanding of the classification of French wine is vital to your wine knowledge, since France long ago invented the wines that the rest of the world imitates. (Even the bottle shapes of the different wine styles and wine regions of France are imitated by California winemakers to indicate the intended style of wine.)

Label law is of particular importance to the classification of French wine. Following is a breakdown of the most important labeling designations from France:

- **Appellation d'Origine Contrôlée (AOC or AC):** This is the most widely applied standard used on French wine labels. It indicates that the wine meets the legal standards (per French wine law) for the area indicated. The more specific the area of origin, the higher the standards.
- **Vin Délimité de Qualité Supérieure (VDQS):** This second set of standards is used for wines in areas not covered by AOC law. Although wines labeled as such are a notch lower in quality, VDQS is still a reliable government guarantee.
- **Vin de Pays:** This indicates "country" wine from outlying areas. Most varietal wines (those wines where the name of the grape is on the bottle) fall under this heading. Sometimes a wine from an AOC may be "declassified" to a *Vin de Pays* in order to meet government regulations pertaining to maximum crop yields. Such a wine, often priced well under $10, is usually a terrific bargain.

In order to understand France's system of wine production, think of the country in terms of its seven major regions. Each of these regions has its own system of organization and classification:

Alsace   Languedoc
Bordeaux   Loire
Burgundy (Bourgogne) Rhône
Champagne

Bordeaux

Bordeaux, an industrial city in Southwestern France, is the center of the world's most famous wine region. Several types of wine are produced here:

- **Dry white wines:** These include blends of Sauvignon Blanc and Sémillon.
- **Sweet dessert wines:** This encompasses blends of Sauvignon Blanc, Sémillon, and Muscadelle afflicted with *botrytis cinerea* (noble rot), the grape mold that concentrates the natural sugars.
- **Medium-bodied red wines:** This classification is comprised of blends of Cabernet Sauvignon, Merlot, Cabernet Franc, Malbec, and Petit Verdot. Some subregions produce wine made primarily from Cabernet Sauvignon, whereas the Merlot grape is dominant in other areas.

There are several subregions of Bordeaux that produce particular types of wine. Here are the most important:

- **Sauternes:** sweet dessert wines
- **Pomerol:** Merlot-dominant reds
- **Saint-Émilion:** Merlot-dominant reds, blended with a significant amount of Cabernet Franc
- **Entre-Deux-Mers:** light, simple whites
- **Graves:** fine dry whites, Cabernet Sauvignon–based reds
- **Médoc:** Cabernet Sauvignon–based reds

The Médoc, a subregion of Bordeaux, is a relatively large area and contains four "communes" (wine-producing areas that are like small towns). These communes are entitled to their own appellation:

Margaux
Pauillac
Saint-Estèphe
Saint-Julien

You will find a great number of châteaux-bottled Bordeaux wines on the market. A château is literally a piece of land. In anticipation of an agricultural exposition in 1855, the local government in Bordeaux asked representatives of the wine trade to rate the red wines of Médoc according to price history. Those wines that had fetched the highest prices over time were given the highest ranking, and so on down. The highest ranking, *Premier Cru* ("first growth"), includes only five (originally four) châteaux, one of which (Château Haut-Brion) is actually from neighboring Graves. This château was included because of its record of excellence. The classified growths of Médoc are ranked first growth, second, third, fourth, and fifth. Below this level are the *Cru Bourgeois* wines and the *Petit Châteaux* wines.

The sweet dessert wines of Sauternes were classified at the time of those of Médoc. Other subregions of Bordeaux have since adopted some form of classification. Although such quality classifications might become outdated and might no longer reflect reality, they can be self-fulfilling prophecies: A *Premier Cru* is expected to be expensive and excellent; therefore, the winemaker can afford to make such a wine, knowing that the market will accept the price.

Burgundy (Bourgogne)
This region begins approximately 62 miles (100 kilometers) south of Paris and stretches about 224 miles (360

kilometers) down to Lyon. Burgundy produces three general types of wine:

1. Light, velvety red wine made from Pinot Noir.
2. Light, fruity red wine made from Gamay.
3. Dry white wine made from Chardonnay.

Although there are other wines made in Burgundy, these are the most important.

If you were to travel from north to south through the heart of France, you would pass through the following subregions of Burgundy in sequence:

- **Chablis:** This subregion produces very dry white wines.
- **Côte de Nuits:** This area is home to full-bodied Pinot Noir reds and also a few whites.
- **Côte de Beaune:** This section is known for its lighter Pinot Noir and excellent Chardonnay.

- **Côte Chalonnaise:** Less expensive Pinot Noir and Chardonnay is produced in this subregion.
- **Mâcon:** Chardonnay whites, including the famous Pouill-Fuissé, are produced here.
- **Beaujolais:** Gamay reds come from this part of Burgundy.

Many of these subregions have their own ranking systems. For instance, the Chablis vineyards are ranked (in descending order of quality) as Chablis *Grand Cru*, Chablis *Premier Cru*, Chablis, and Petit Chablis. The red and white vineyards of the Côte de Nuits and Côte de Beaune (together known as the Côte-d'Or) are ranked either *Grand Cru* or *Premier Cru*, although sometimes they are not ranked at all.

Some of Burgundy's subregions break down further into other sections. For example, the famous villages of the Côte de Nuits are Nuits-Saint-Georges; Gevrey-Chambertin; Vosne-Romanée; Morey-Saint-Denis; and Chambolle-Musigny. These villages are all well known for their red wines, some of which are fabulously expensive.

The Côte de Beaune encompasses an even greater number of renowned villages, known for producing either red or white wine. According to wine type, these are:

REDS

Beaune	Pommard
Meursault	Savigny-lès-Beaune
Pernand-Vergelesses	Volnay

WHITES

Beaune	Meursault
Chassagne-Montrachet	Puligny-Montrachet
Aloxe-Corton	

Beaujolais is the southernmost subregion of Burgundy. However, the Pinot Noir grape of the Côte-d'Or (and Côte Chalonnaise) gives way to the Gamay grape, which produces charming wines in Beaujolais' granite-rich soil.

The wines of Beaujolais may be labeled as Beaujolais, Beaujolais Supérieur (which is 1 percent higher in alcohol content than simple Beaujolais), Beaujolais-Villages, or *cru* Beaujolais with a village name. Moulin-à-Vent, Brouilly, and Saint-Amour are the best known of the *crus*. There are ten such *cru* villages entitled to use their own names. *Cru* Beaujolais is the best of the Beaujolais and, since it usually costs less than $15 a bottle, it's quite a bargain!

Rhône

Earthy, gutsy wines, both red and white, are produced along the Rhône River, which lies south of the Burgundy region. Mercifully, the wines of the Rhône region do not have a ranking system.

Northern Rhône reds include:

Big, Syrah-based reds worthy of aging for at least a few years.
Cornas
Côte-Rôtie
Crozes-Hermitage
Saint-Joseph

Northern Rhône whites are substantial wines made from Viognier or a blend of Marsanne and Roussane. These include:

Condrieu
Crozes-Hermitage

The following red wines are produced in Southern Rhône:

Grenache-based blends (with Syrah, Cinsault, Mourvédre, and other grapes)
Côtes du Rhône
Gigondas
Châteauneuf-du-Pape

Although not so common, Southern Rhône whites are big wines made from Marsanne and Roussane. These wines are an interesting alternative to Chardonnay:

Côtes du Rhône Blanc
Châteauneuf-du-Pape Blanc

The Southern Rhône region also produces a distinguished rosé known as Tavel. This dry rosé, made primarily from Grenache, is considered by many wine buffs to be the finest rosé in the world.

Loire

The vineyards along the largest river in France yield a variety of refreshing (mostly white) wines. Here are the most important ones:

* **Muscadet:** A perfect shellfish wine, it is made from the grape of the same name.
* **Vouvray:** Produced from the Chenin Blanc grape, Vouvray can be bone-dry (sec), delightfully off-dry (demi-sec), or sparkling.
* **Rosé d'Anjou:** This off-dry rosé is made mostly from the Grolleau grape, while superior rosés from the region made from Cabernet Sauvignon and Cabernet Franc are labeled Cabernet d'Anjou.
* **Pouilly-Fumé:** A straight Sauvignon Blanc with a rich, heady style, this wine is the inspiration for California Sauvignon Blancs labeled "Fumé Blanc."
* **Sancerre:** This unblended Sauvignon Blanc is more acidic than Pouilly-Fumé.

Alsace

Historically, ownership of the geographical area of Alsace has flip-flopped back and forth between Germany and France, according to which country claimed victory in the most recent war. As such, although Alsace is currently a part of France, considerable German influence is, nevertheless, apparent in this region's wines. Late harvest, sweet wines are produced in Alsace.

In this region, there is a tradition of varietal labeling: No "cutting" is allowed. If a wine is named according to grape variety, then it must be made only from that grape. The term *Grand Cru* may appear on an Alsace label as an indication that the wine has a minimum alcohol content of 10 or 11 percent (depending on the grape) and meets some perfunctory yield requirements. The varieties used in Alsace wines are:

Riesling
Sylvaner
Gewürztraminer
Pinot Gris (Tokay Pinot Gris)
A small amount of Pinot Noir (the only red, Muscat often used for rosé)

Champagne

In order to qualify for the Champagne appellation (according to French and EEC law), a sparkling wine must:

1. Be produced in the Champagne district
2. Be produced from the Chardonnay, Pinot Noir, and/or Pinot Meunier (red) grapes grown there
3. Get its bubbles via the méthode champenoise (Champagne method)

The Champagne method is an expensive and labor-intensive means of naturally carbonating a wine. First, wine is made from local grapes. This is no easy feat; the vineyards of Champagne lie so far north that ripeness is an issue in most years. After clarification and aging, the wine is put into thick Champagne bottles, along with enough yeast and sugar to initiate a second fermentation. It is this second fermentation in the tightly sealed bottle that puts the bubbles in the bubbly—the carbon dioxide cannot escape, so it is dissolved in the wine.

Then comes the hard work—removing the dead yeast. After aging the wine with the dead yeast—sometimes for many years, as this adds character to the Champagne—the dead yeast is then coaxed into the neck of the bottle by gradually tilting the bottle a little bit each day until it is inverted. The dead yeast is then carefully removed. At this time, the bottle is topped off and adjusted for sweetness. Champagnes can vary significantly in terms of sweetness, and the amount of sugar is noted on the bottle's label. Following are the distinctions used to indicate Champagne's sweetness:

- **Natural or Au Sauvage** indicates no sugar has been added.
- **Brut** is the designation used for very dry Champagne that contains no more than 1.5 percent sugar by volume.
- **Extra Dry** Champagne contains up to 2 percent sugar.
- **Dry or Sec** Champagne contains up to 4 percent sugar.
- **Demi-Sec** Champagne is sweeter, with as much as 8 percent sugar.
- **Doux** Champagne is very sweet and consists of up to 10 percent sugar.

When considering champagne, there are some other important terms with which you should be familiar. These include:

- **Blanc de Blancs:** This term indicates that a champagne is made only from white grapes, such as Chardonnay.
- **Brut Rosé:** This is a designation used for pink-colored Champagne. The color is derived from the red skins of Pinot Noir and/or Pinot Meunier grapes.
- **Blanc de Noirs:** Pale sparkling wine from dark-skinned grapes goes by this label.
- **Téte de Cuvée:** This term is used to distinguish a super premium Champagne, usually vintage dated.
- **Vintage:** In contrast to the far more common practice of blending wines from different years, vintage Champagne is made from the wine of a single harvest. Although most téte de cuvées are vintage dated, a year on the bottle doesn't mean that it is superior to a nonvintage bottle.

Italy

For a beginning wine lover becoming familiar with the wines of France and their Californian counterparts, the world of Italian wine can be a tough nut to crack. Although the wines of the United States can be explained in relation to their French counterparts (and *vice versa*), the wines of Italy cannot. The land we now call Italy has been producing wine for 4,000 years; however, Italy was not politically unified within its present borders until the mid-1800s. This land of diverse climates, cultures, and dialects produces a baffling variety of wines.

The wines of Italy rival those of France in variety, quantity, and, in many cases, quality. Like France, Italy more often than not labels her wines according to geographical origin rather than grape variety. (Of course, as with France, there are exceptions.) Italy is divided politically into twenty regions. From south to north, these include:

Calabria (the "toe")
Abruzzo
Latium (*Lazio*)
Apulia (*Puglia* in Italian, also known as the "heel")
Umbria
Basilicata
Marche
Campania
Tuscany (*Toscana*)
Molise
Emilia-Romagna

In the north, there are also several regions along the French, Swiss, Austrian, and Slovenian borders. These are:

Liguria
Trentino-Alto Adige
Piedmont (*Piemonte*)
Veneto
Valle d'Aosta
Friuli-Venezia Giulia
Lombardy (*Lombardia*)

There are two island regions as well:

Sicily (*Sicilia,* right off the coast of the Calabria region)
Sardinia (about 200 miles off the coast of the Latium region)

Sardinia and Sicily

Italy is a wine-loving country, and every one of these regions produces wine. The island region of Sardinia, for instance, which is dedicated primarily to other forms of agriculture such as sheep and cattle, nonetheless produces interesting wines. In particular, the white grape Vermentino yields a light and crisp hot-weather wine. Meanwhile, the other island region, Sicily, has half a million acres of vineyards and has traditionally produced a variety of powerful, deeply colored red wines as well as a few whites. Ample Sicilian sunshine and warmth encourage viticulture on hillsides not quite fertile or rainy enough for abundant cultivation of other crops, though Sicily is certainly a bountiful garden compared to cooler wine regions in Northern Europe. Presently, the Nero d'Avola grape, native to Sicily, is enjoying a renaissance in the hands of modern producers, and better-known grape varieties—even Chardonnay—have performed well.

Calabria and Apulia

Across the narrow Strait of Messina, the sun-drenched Calabria region barely dabbles in viticulture, devoting its rocky terrain instead to other forms of agriculture such as olives, eggplants, and lemons. However, the neighboring Apulia region, with its minerally, vine-friendly terrain, is a far more important wine producing region, if only in quantity. Its vineyard acreage equals Sicily's, and Primitivo di Manduria—the Italian version of the Zinfandel grape—as well as the rustic, inexpensive Salice Salentino are two Apulian red wines that regularly appear in American wine stores.

Campania

The Campania region is the source of Southern Italy's finest wines. The Aglianico grape, also grown in the neighboring Basilicata region where it is bottled as Aglianico del Vulture, yields a fine red wine in Campania's volcanic hillsides. The finest vintages of Aglianico, when vinified by

Campania's top producers in the Taurasi zone, are among the greatest wines of Italy. Less noble grapes, such as the white varieties Coda di Volpe and Greco and the red Piedirosso, also perform well in Campanian vineyards.

Abruzzo

The Abruzzo region, on Italy's east coast, produces an ocean of inexpensive red wine confusingly named Montepulciano d'Abruzzo. Here we have "Montepulciano" used as the name of a grape variety, while it is also the name of a famous wine district in the Tuscany region. Montepulciano d'Abruzzo, at $6 to $10 per bottle, has become the quintessential "pizza wine"; however, *riserva* bottlings, made from vineyards with old vines and severely limited yields, can approach the greatness of the more famous Italian treasures from Campania and the northern regions.

Umbria

The neighboring Umbria region in Central Italy has enjoyed relatively recent success with varietal Sangiovese and Merlot, while a high-quality, indigenous red grape is bottled as Sagrantino di Montefalco, well-made versions of which will reward a decade of cellar aging. It's not hard to understand why Umbrian wine producers have developed an inferiority complex over the centuries—Umbria's neighbor to the northwest is Tuscany, one of the very finest wine regions in the world.

Tuscany

A tour of Tuscan wines begins in the Chianti district. Many wine drinkers associate Chianti with the cheap, straw-wrapped bottles of indifferent quality sold for many years in

American wine stores. Today, these bottles are increasingly scarce. The Chianti region, famous for its food-friendly wine, has recently solidified its reputation as a fine wine–producing subregion of Tuscany. Here, the Sangiovese grape and its close relatives thrive in the calcium-rich soils and moderate climate. The Chianti area is divided into seven zones:

Chianti Classico
Chianti Colli Aretini
Chianti Colli Fiorentini
Chianti Colli Senesi
Chianti Colline Pisane
Chianti Montalbano
Chianti Rufina

Of these, only Classico, Rufina, and perhaps Colli Senesi can be readily found in wine stores. Wine labeled simply as "Chianti" might well be from an outlying vineyard in the district. To the south of the Chianti district, there are two other fine wine–producing areas: the towns of Montepulciano and Montalcino.

The sandy, well-drained vineyards of Montepulciano yield a red wine known as Vino Nobile di Montepulciano, a Sangiovese-based wine somewhat richer than that produced in Chianti, due in part to Montepulciano's slightly warmer microclimate. In Montalcino, meanwhile, a microclimate even warmer and drier yet brings a sturdier clone of Sangiovese—the Sangiovese Grosso, or "Brunello" grape—to lush, full ripeness. This wine is bottled as Brunello di Montalcino. Both Vino Nobile di Montepulciano and Brunello di Montalcino have "little brothers"— Rosso di Montepulciano and Rosso di Montalcino. Easier to confuse with each other than with their older brothers, they are generally light-bodied and relatively inexpensive reds intended for early consumption.

The Northernmost Regions

The Italian regions in the foothills of the Alps are home to many grape varieties, some familiar and others barely known outside of their regions. The Trentino-Alto Adige region sits along the Austrian border. Though it is one region, Trentino is the southern, Italian-speaking part while German is spoken in Alto Adige. Considering its northerly latitude (46°N), the region is surprisingly warm, as warm air accumulates on the south side of the Alps. As such, internationally known grape varieties—the usual suspects—ripen easily and can be produced in large quantities. Chardonnay, Pinot Nero (Pinot Noir), Cabernet Sauvignon, Merlot, Pinot Bianco, and the ubiquitous Pinot Grigio are among the seventeen varieties bottled by name, as are the lesser-known local red grapes Schiava, Lagrein, and Teroldego.

Likewise, the Friuli region, in northeastern Italy, can ripen a wide variety of *vinifera* grapes, albeit with a tilt in the direction of fresh, fruity whites produced in its geologically wine-friendly hillsides and plains. Meanwhile, the Veneto region, situated between Friuli and Trentino-Alto Adige, produces a diverse assortment of wines. Soave, Bardolino, Valpolicella, Prosecco . . . these names fill the Italian racks at the wine store, and they all come from the Veneto region, which is a close third behind Apulia and Sicily in total wine production.

Prosecco is a delightfully clean and crisp sparkler produced in bulk from the grape of the same name. It's widely available in the $8 to $12 range. The Veneto region produces a considerable amount of inexpensive wines labeled by grape variety. Just about every region in Italy, from Sicily to Friuli, bottles its own version of Pinot Grigio, and the Veneto certainly contributes its share.

The Piave river valley in eastern Veneto is an especially prolific source of inexpensive, varietal Merlot, as well as other varietals.

Soave, the best-known white wine of the Veneto region, is a blend based on the local Garganega grape. The house of Bolla made Soave something of a brand name in the 1970s with its mass-produced and mass-marketed version of the wine, yet there are several distinctive versions available from small producers. The Soave district's nextdoor neighbors, the Bardolino and Valpolicella districts, are hosts to similarly mass-produced reds. Both Bardolino and Valpolicella are made from blends of grapes featuring the Corvina grape. Their normally light body is a reflection of the high crop yields commonly associated with mass production. As with Soave, there are some intriguing, handcrafted counterexamples.

At the other end of the spectrum in the Valpolicella district of the Veneto region is Amarone, another of Italy's wine treasures. A relatively recent development in fine Italian wine, Amarone is made in the same district and from the same grapes as common Valpolicella. However, the grapes used for Amarone are dried on straw mats for up to four months, a process that reduces the grapes' water content and, thus, concentrates the sugars. The resulting wine is richly flavored and textured with an alcoholic content of perhaps 15 to 16 percent. Like others in the pantheon of great Italian wines, Amarone is capable of aging for several decades. Next to a rich and powerful Amarone, plain Valpolicella can seem downright watery. However, some Valpolicella producers referment their wine with sediment left over from Amarone fermentation. This method of "repassing" (*ripasso*) Valpolicella gives it additional richness and complexity.

Piedmont

Veneto's Amarone, along with Taurasi from Campania and the many excellent wines from Tuscany, have earned their place among the world's great wines. However, of Italy's twenty wine regions, most connoisseurs would agree that the very finest Italian wines come from Piedmont. Nebbiolo is one of the noblest *vinifera* varieties, yet it accomplishes little beyond the borders of Piedmont. However, in the vineyards of Barolo and Barbaresco, the Nebbiolo grape attains a degree of greatness shared only with the world's finest examples of Cabernet Sauvignon, Pinot Noir, Syrah, and perhaps Sangiovese. Although there is a degree of geological diversity in the region, the Piedmontese soils in which Nebbiolo thrives are not unlike those in Burgundy, where Pinot Noir grows so beautifully. This soil has mixtures of limestone, clay, and, in some areas, a proportion of sandstone as well.

The Nebbiolo grape gets its name from *nebbia*, the autumn fog prevalent in Piedmont. The region's subalpine climate—hot summers and relatively mild autumn days—brings the Nebbiolo, as well as the lesser varieties, to ideal ripeness. While Nebbiolo is a late-ripening variety, the Barbera grape ripens a little earlier and yields a low-tannin, high-acid red with broad appeal. The Dolcetto grape, which ripens even earlier, makes an almost Beaujolais-like light red perfect for youthful consumption. Lesser-known native grape varieties include Brachetto, Freisa, and Grignolino.

While Piedmont is best known for its outstanding reds, the white Gavi, made from the native Cortese variety, is a crisp and minerally seafood wine not unlike a good Sauvignon Blanc. In contrast, the Arneis grape can produce a less acidic, overtly fruity white meant for early consumption.

Piedmont also produces a few different sparkling wines. The mass-produced Asti Spumante is known worldwide as a sweet and inexpensive alternative to more serious sparklers, while the more refined Moscato d'Asti is less alcoholic (only 5.5 percent) and less effervescent. It also has a red cousin: Brachetto d'Acqui is a sweet, low-alcohol, slightly sparkling red with an aroma of fresh strawberries as festive as Moscato d'Asti's floral Muscat scent.

The Italian government recognizes the traditional wines of Italy (as well as some newcomers) with a system similar to France:

- **Denominazione di Origine Controllata e Garantita (DOCG):** This is the highest status conferred on Italian wines. It guarantees that the wine is of a traditional style from its region; made from specified grape varieties grown at the proper crop levels; and aged for a specified period of time prior to release. For example, Brunello di Montalcino, a DOCG wine from Tuscany, must be made from the Sangiovese Grosso clone (a.k.a. "Brunello") of the Sangiovese grape and is aged for four years prior to release.
- **Denominazione di Origine Controllata (DOC):** This next-highest level is often found on "little brother" wines, such as Tuscany's Rosso di Montalcino, the "little brother" of Brunello di Montalcino.
- **Indicazione Geografica Tipica (IGT):** This is a category for wines, some of which might include innovative styles or varieties that do not conform to DOCG/DOC regulations. For example, this includes varietals such as Syrah from Tuscany. IGT wine labels must indicate the general region of origin.

- **Vino da Tavola (VdT):** "Table wine," just like the French *vin de table*, is the general category for non-DOC/DOCG wines of indistinct origin. Before the IGT category was instituted, the high-quality, innovative "super-Tuscan" wines were labeled as VdT wines.

Major Italian Wine Types

Color	Type of Wine	Region	Grape Varieties
Red	Barolo	Piedmont	Nebbiolo
Red	Barbaresco	Piedmont	Nebbiolo
Red	Valpolicella	Veneto	Corvina, Rondinella, and Molinara
Red	Amarone	Veneto	Corvina, Rondinella, and Molinara
Red	Barbera d'Asti	Piedmont	Barbera
Red	Chianti	Tuscany	Mostly Sangiovese
Red	Brunello di Montalcino	Tuscany	Brunello (a grape closely related to Sangiovese)
Red	Piave Merlot	Veneto	Merlot
Red	Morellino di Scansano	Tuscany	Mostly Sangiovese
Red	Taurasi	Campania	Aglianico and Piedirosso
Red	Salice Salentino	Puglia	Negro amaro
White	Soave	Veneto	Garganega and Trebbiano
White	Gavi	Piedmont	Cortese
White	Orvieto	Umbria	Trebbiano, Verdello, and Grechetto
White	Greco di Tufo	Campania	Greco and Coda di Volpe

Germany

While Chardonnay-based wines are far more familiar to the American public, Rieslings, especially those from Germany, are just as good. When people think of German wines, they usually think of Riesling. But Germany has other wines of distinction as well.

German wine has not played a significant role in the United States wine boom, probably for a few different reasons. First of all, Californian versions of Riesling haven't been so great. Because of this, Americans aren't inspired to "go to the source" as they have done for other grapes. Although many consumers who've been hooked by Californian Chardonnay experiment with the French Chardonnays of Burgundy, not so with German Rieslings.

Second, German wines have a reputation for being too sweet. Although many of Germany's wines are less dry than Americans prefer, Germany does make some wonderful dry Riesling. Liebfraumilch, an overrated and somewhat sweet wine, was briefly in vogue in the states in the late 1960s and early '70s. This wine is partly responsible for the misconception that German wine equals sweet wine.

When people look at the indecipherable German wine labels on today's wines, many wonder if they are looking at a Liebfraumilch-type wine. Perhaps if people understood the labels on the bottles, they would be more willing to experiment with German wines.

Following is a list to help you decipher those labels. Like the other European Union countries, Germany has a government-regulated wine-rating system. Of the three levels of quality, the top two are exported to the United States. The levels are:

- **Qualitätswein mit Prädikat (QmP):** This description is used for the highest-quality wine.
- **Qualitätswein bestimmter Anbaugebiete (QbA):** This is the designation for middle-quality wine.
- **Tafelwein:** This is the lowest-level wine.

QbA indicates quality wine from a quality region. Unless the label specifies that the wine is a Riesling, then it is made from another variety or, more likely, varieties. Other common German varieties are:

Sylvaner
Müller-Thurgau (a cross between Riesling and Sylvaner)
Gewürztraminer

Because QmP is the designation of highest quality, QmP wine labels offer more information about the wine. The Prädikats, or levels of distinction, indicate the sugar level at harvest. Because Germany's vineyards are so far north, it is difficult to get the grapes to ripen, hence grape sugars are highly prized. Chaptalization, the addition of sugars to increase the alcohol content via fermentation, is not allowed in QmP wines.

The Prädikats, or distinctions, are as follows:

- **Kabinett:** Normal, fully ripe grapes (9.5 percent minimum potential alcohol).
- **Spätlese:** "Late-harvested" grapes, which may produce slightly sweet wine.
- **Auslese:** Individually selected, very ripe bunches used to make sweet wine.
- **Beerenauslese:** Individually selected, very ripe grapes ("berries") used to make extremely sweet dessert wine.
- **Trockenbeerenauslese:** Individually selected, *botrytis* afflicted grapes used to make the sweetest, most expensive German dessert wines.
- **Eiswein (icewine):** A relatively new Prädikat reserved for wines that are made from grapes naturally frozen

on the vine and pressed while frozen. This method concentrates sugar, as much of the grape's water is left behind as ice crystals.

Look for the word *trocken* on your German wine label as well; this means dry. *Halbtrocken* means half-dry.

QmP Kabinett and Spätlese wines are as complex and delicious as Chardonnays in the $12 to $18 price range. A growing trend in German wine is varietal-labeled Riesling QbA wines. At $8 to $10, these wines represent a very good value and match well with Asian cuisine because their touch of sweetness puts out the spicy fire.

Wine Wisdom

Germany enjoys a healthy sparkling-wine industry. German bubbly, known as Sekt, is quite different from French and Californian sparkling wines, which are usually made from Chardonnay and Pinot Noir. Sekt is produced from Riesling and other German varieties, and it can be of high quality when produced by the Champagne method.

Of the many wine-producing areas in Germany, the two most outstanding are the Mosel-Saar-Ruwer region (along the Mosel River and its two tributaries), and the three contiguous regions along the Rhine River:

Rheingau
Rheinhessen
Rheinpfalz

The Riesling grape is the top grape in both areas. Fine Mosel Riesling tends to have mineral and citrus notes, with the classic Riesling floral bouquet. Rhine Riesling is usually richer, with apricot-like fruit. These rival areas distinguish themselves by bottle color: bright green for Mosel wines, brown for Rhines.

Spain

Spain has a history of wine production as old as that of France, yet her wines are not nearly as well known to American consumers. With a hot and dry climate, Spain seems like the perfect place to bring grapes to full ripeness. However, the scientific and technological developments that have improved European winemaking over the centuries have had little influence on the Spanish wine industry until very recently. Modern Spanish winemaking is presently undergoing a quality boom, and a variety of affordable, world-class reds as well as a few interesting whites are joining Sherry and inexpensive Spanish sparkling wine (Cava) on our store shelves.

As noted in Chapter 2, "Sherry" is the anglicized name of the southeastern Spanish city of Jerez de la Frontera and has long been Spain's best and most famous wine. The white Palomino grape develops delicacy and finesse in the chalky soils of the legally defined Jerez district, even though the district's withering heat would make soup of most fine grape varieties. Unfortunately, the wine boom of the last three decades hasn't done much for Sherry; if anything, newly converted wine enthusiasts tend to view Sherry as a manufactured product quite distinct from fine wine, and Port is most often their fortified wine of choice. (Also see Chapter 2 for a detailed explanation of Sherry production.)

Rioja

The Rioja region in North-Central Spain was one of the few beneficiaries of *phylloxera* and other vineyard scourges of the 1800s. Many French winemakers and merchants became suddenly unemployed when the vineyards of France were struck down, first by mildew and later by *phylloxera*, and a number of them set up shop in the Rioja region right over the Pyrenees Mountains from Southern France. The red wines of Rioja, made from the Tempranillo and Garnacha (Grenache) varieties, were greatly improved by the Gallic influence and quickly gained favor in France.

Catalonia

Unlike many of Spain's wine regions, which roast in high summer temperatures and struggle for sufficient water (irrigation is forbidden in Spain), the region of Catalonia along the Mediterranean coast enjoys a climate moderated by its proximity to the sea. This is the seat of the gigantic Spanish sparkling wine industry, whose famous producers include the twin giants Freixenet and Codorniu. "Cava," as Spanish sparkling wine is known, is produced by the Champagne method from lesser-known, native white grape varieties such as Macabeo and Xarel-lo. (The Champagne region's Chardonnay grape was only approved for Cava production in 1986.)

Priorato

The summer temperatures just a few miles inland from the Mediterranean coast are quite warm, and the Catalonian subregion of Priorato has all the makings of a first-rate (if tiny) wine district: relentless sun, stony soils nearly incapable of supporting other vegetation, and a renewed interest from modern winemakers, who use French barrels and have planted better-known red varieties such as Cabernet Sauvignon and Syrah to complement the indigenous Garnacha and Cariñena (the French Carignane). Some truly world-class red wines displaying both muscle and elegance have emerged from Priorato in recent years, and great things are expected of this region in the near future.

Ribera del Duero

Important wine regions throughout the world are often distinguished by a river, and one of the world's great wine rivers rises in the central Spanish highlands north of Madrid. Downstream, in Portugal, it is known as the Douro, the home of the port industry, but in Spain it is called the Duero. Along its upland banks, the Ribera del Duero wine region is challenging the nearby Rioja area for supremacy among Spanish wine regions. Although the Ribera del Duero region bakes in merciless Spanish sunshine by day, cool nighttime temperatures associated with this location's high altitude keep acid levels in the grapes at an acceptable level. Red wine from Ribera del Duero is produced from the Tinto Fino grape, a close relative of the Tempranillo variety.

Noteworthy Whites from Spain

There are few Spanish dry white wines of importance. White Rioja, made from the native Viura grape, can be pleasant for fans of oaky flavors, and there is a growing amount of varietal Chardonnay and other internationally marketable varieties being produced in the Catalonian subregion of Penedès. Perhaps the most distinctive Spanish white wine on the market today is varietal Albariño, produced near the Atlantic coast to the north of Portugal. Due to its thick skins, Albariño makes a heavy wine, often reminiscent of the Rhône's Viogniers. As such, it can be an interesting antidote to Chardonnay fatigue.

Portugal

Portugal is, perhaps, the last bastion of truly old-world winemaking. Here, wine estates have thus far refused to uproot their native varieties in order to stick Chardonnay and Merlot vines in the ground. There is a downside to this rare and admirable respect for past tradition, however. The world of Portuguese table wine is a maze of unrecognizable grape varieties and obscure place-names. Port, produced in the Douro valley, is the "winiest" of the world's fortified wines and is well known to American wine drinkers. (A full treatment of Port is given in Chapter 2.) Perhaps the Portuguese table wines best known to American consumers are the twin rosés Mateus and Lancer's, which were wildly popular a few decades ago at the beginning of the wine boom.

Vinho Verde—"green wine"—is produced from native grape varieties and vinified in a distinctively food-friendly style—sharply dry and acidic, low in alcohol, and slightly fizzy. Portuguese reds, impenetrable as their labels may be, are often the best values around for fans of puckery dry, rustic wines under $10. Portugal is not without its expensive treasures, however. The most highly acclaimed Portuguese red table wines come from the Douro River valley and are made from the same grapes used for Port production. The best of these Douro reds command prices similar to those of highly rated Californian reds.

Austria

Austrian wine is quite possibly the most underappreciated treasure in the world of wine today. Perhaps American wine consumers think of Austrian wine as sweet, or it is too easy to confuse Austria with Australia. Or maybe the wine drinkers of today remember the infamous Austrian wine scandal of two decades ago, when some Austrian Trockenbeerenauslese dessert wines were found to contain additives that made them seem thicker than usual. The truth is that the Austrians forcefully responded to that scandal by enacting the most comprehensive (if difficult to understand) body of wine laws in the world, and Austrian wine is held to some of the highest standards in the world for purity, truthful labeling, and quality. Of course, none of this would matter if the wines were not of such high quality to begin with.

Separated from nearby Northern Italian wine regions by the imposing Alps, the vineyards of Eastern Austria, first cultivated by the wine-loving ancient Celts, are blessed with a typically continental climate—hot summer days, cool summer nights, and enough autumn warmth to bring quality wine grapes to full ripeness. In the southeast corner, in the foothills of the Alps, the Styria region produces only a small amount of Austria's wine, albeit of high quality. Chardonnay, known locally as "Morillon," grows in the steep Styrian hillside vineyards, as does Sauvignon Blanc. The Pinot Blanc grape, known locally as Weissburgunder, also performs well in Styria, and so does the red Zweigelt grape, a popular crossing of the alpine red variety St. Laurent with the German Blaufränkisch. To the north of Styria, along the Hungarian border, the Burgenland region partially surrounds Lake Neusiedler See and yields some of the world's greatest dessert wines as well as Austria's boldest reds. However, most of the country's top-quality wines are produced in the northeast corner of Austria, in "Lower Austria," situated along the Danube.

Like the other wine-producing districts of Lower Austria, the Weinviertel produces much of its wine from Austria's own white variety, the Grüner Veltliner grape. And yet, a wide variety of other grapes are grown in the sprawling Weinviertel district, including Chardonnay, Riesling, Weissburgunder, and Sauvignon Blanc among whites, and Zweigelt and even Cabernet Sauvignon among reds. Although the Weinviertel's reputation has long been based on quantity rather than quality, the wines of the district are rapidly improving in the hands of a new generation of winemakers. Farther up the Danube River valley, the districts of Kremstal, Kamtal, and Wachau also produce delicious (if pricier) Grüner Veltliners and brilliant, bone-dry Rieslings, the best of which are among the finest dry white wines in the world.

The United States

Much of the early history of American wine involved a struggle for superiority between the colonial agriculturalists in the East and the relatively recent settlers in California. Although the Eastern states held the early lead, California's supremacy as an American wine-producing region has been unquestionable since the late 1800s. Although wine is now produced in all fifty states, few states besides California successfully produce quality wine on a noteworthy scale. In fact, only Oregon, Washington, and New York produce wines that are consumed beyond their own borders in commercially significant quantities. Many of the wineries in the other states rely heavily on tourist traffic and the accompanying retail wine sales at the winery's door.

California

The sunny hillsides and valleys of Central and Northern California have proved to be ideal locations for bringing *vinifera* varieties—even stubborn ripeners like Cabernet Sauvignon—to lush, full ripeness. This is possible because of California's long, dry, and hot summers.

Shortly after prohibition was repealed, two Californian academics at the University of California at Davis, professors Maynard Amerine and Albert Winkler, devised an ingenious method for classifying Californian wine regions according to their capacity for heat accumulation. The Amerine-Winkler scale is based on the average monthly temperature above 50°F during the growing season from April through October. A "degree-day " is a day with a 24-hour average temperature of 51°F, and, therefore, a single day with an average temperature of 75°F would contribute 25 degree-days to the heat accumulation required for ripening grapes. Amerine and Winkler classified the established wine regions of California in order of increasing heat accumulation, expressed in degree-days:

- **Region I:** Fewer than 2,500 degree-days
- **Region II:** 2,500–3,000
- **Region III:** 3,000–3,500
- **Region IV:** 3,500–4,000
- **Region V:** More than 4,000 degree-days

It is generally true in California as well as the rest of the world that greater heat accumulation makes possible larger crops of grapes. However, as the Romans and French learned, often the finest wines come from cooler vineyard sites where the warmth is spread over a longer ripening period, and grapes must struggle somewhat to achieve full ripeness. And so the finest dry table wines of California are usually produced in the regions I and II, such as the cooler parts of the Napa and Sonoma Valleys, while the hotter regions, like the vast San Joaquin Valley, are better suited to the production of fortified wines, raisins, and table grapes. It follows that there is an ideal balance for a vineyard location: warm enough to bring the grapes to full ripeness at economically rewarding crop levels, yet cool enough to prolong this ripening period in order to allow maximum flavor development. California, particularly Napa Valley, has many such sites.

Napa Valley and Sonoma Valley

Napa Valley has long enjoyed primacy among the wine regions of California, although the others are rapidly closing the gap. Stretching twenty miles north from San Francisco Bay, Napa Valley is characterized by a hot valley floor, cooler hillsides and mountaintops, and world-class Cabernet Sauvignon. Napa Chardonnay is also a star, and Napa versions of heat-loving, old-vine Zinfandel and Petite Sirah can be excellent. Unfortunately, the Napa region has evolved into a Mecca of spas, resorts, and mansions, and the skyrocketing real estate prices in Napa Valley have helped to drive up wine prices.

Sonoma Valley, meanwhile, has lagged behind Napa Valley in both wine accolades and gentrification. While Sonoma certainly turns out its share of quality Cabernet Sauvignon, the cooler coastal areas of Sonoma have proved to be a reliable source of some of the state's finest Chardonnay. These Sonoma subregions are also noteworthy for their Pinot Noir, a noble variety that fails to thrive in Napa Valley's warmth. Likewise, the Carneros district—the southernmost tip of both Napa and Sonoma Counties—is a perfect venue for Pinot Noir and other heat-shy grapes.

The Central Coast

The Santa Cruz mountain area south of San Francisco Bay was the cradle of nineteenth-century fine wine production in California. In this area, Paul Masson and Charles LeFranc cultivated newly imported, premium grape varieties from France. Today the vast "Central Coast" region of central California, stretching from the Santa Cruz Mountains south to Santa Barbara, is rapidly becoming known for a wide variety of fine wines, from Chardonnay and Pinot Noir in the coastal draws and on mountaintops, to Zinfandel and Cabernet Sauvignon in Paso Robles. Rhône varieties such as Syrah, Grenache, and Viognier are also grown in several subregions by the innovative "Rhône Rangers."

The Pacific Northwest

The Pacific Northwest may actually be on equal footing with California in certain aspects of wine production. While any overview of wine production in the United States must focus on California, the wines of the Pacific Northwest cannot be ignored. California is among the finest wine regions in the world—a region that produces more high-quality wine than most wine-producing *countries*. However, not all grape varieties thrive in its warmth, and the Pacific Northwest with its cooler growing areas complements California perfectly. Quality wines from popular grape varieties come from Oregon and Washington. Although these states combined produce far less wine than the state of California, the Pacific Northwest actually enjoys some advantages over California when it comes to production.

One factor is rooted in economics. The wine boom has driven the price of California vineyard acreage sky-high, which, in turn, has inflated production costs. This is why Washington State Merlot is often the equal of similarly priced Californian versions. Another factor is the climate. Although the Californian sun ripens grapes with ease, the Yakima and Columbia Valleys of Washington, while somewhat cooler than California's Napa and Sonoma Valleys, enjoy more hours of summer sunshine because of their more northerly latitude. The relentless warmth and sunshine in California's Napa Valley might be perfect for Cabernet Sauvignon, but other premium red varieties—namely, Merlot and Syrah—require a little less heat accumulation to ripen properly. Cooler temperatures allow these earlier-ripening red grape varieties to ripen at an optimum pace and develop full, complex flavors, while the longer hours of sunshine provide them sufficient heat accumulation. Cabernet Sauvignon, meanwhile, also performs well in this Washington State climate, but with less power and more finesse than its Napa Valley counterparts.

While California certainly produces enough Chardonnay to go around, there are many fine Washington State versions of this ubiquitous variety from the Pacific Northwest. Washington State also excels in the production of Riesling, a cool-climate variety that doesn't perform so well in California's high temperatures. If the Washington State wine regions are on par with California's—in quality, if not quantity—it can be said that the cool vineyards of Oregon have some definite advantages over California's warm valleys.

California winemakers, so successful with heat-loving Cabernet Sauvignon, struggled for many decades with their Pinot Noirs before finally seeking cooler terrain. In the early 1960s, pioneering winemaker David Lett and others recognized Pinot Noir's affinity for the cool and cloudy climate in Oregon's Willamette Valley. Today, Oregon Pinot Noirs are often described as "Burgundian"—a tasting note rarely associated with the often-overripe Californian versions. Perhaps the highest compliment ever paid to Oregon Pinot Noir comes from the venerable Burgundy wine producer Joseph Drouhin. The Drouhin family considered Oregon Pinot Noir to be of such high quality—especially after they watched Oregon wines defeat their own in a blind tasting—that they purchased vineyard land in the Willamette Valley and started producing their own Oregon Pinot Noir. Today, Domaine Drouhin "Cuvée Laurène" is considered to be among the finest American Pinot Noirs.

Pinot Gris is the other success story in Oregon. This grape variety, also grown in Alsace and Italy, grows best in a cool climate such as Oregon's. California winemakers have yet to click with this variety, but Oregon Pinot Gris at its best is comparable to the fine versions from Alsace, France.

New York

New York State, another cool-climate wine region, was once a major wine-producing state. In recent years, this region has redefined itself. The Finger Lakes district, established in the 1860s, was based on the production of wine from native North American grape varieties and native/French hybrids, vineyard stock capable of withstanding the brutal northeastern winters. It was only a matter of time, however, before the new railroads enabled the Californian wine industry to overtake the wineries of the Eastern states, and New York's domestic market steadily dwindled.

Then, in the 1950s, Dr. Konstantin Frank, a Russian-born German who immigrated to the United States after World War II, began successfully planting *vinifera* varieties in the Finger Lakes region. His success with Chardonnay, Gewürztraminer, and especially Riesling encouraged other widespread plantings. Today, the Finger Lakes region is enjoying a rebirth. There are suddenly dozens of small, hands-on producers—no doubt the beneficiaries of retail sales at their wineries—who produce excellent and affordable Rieslings that are drier and more full-bodied than their German cousins.

The New York State fine wine industry is not confined to the Finger Lakes. Winemakers on the North Fork of Long Island, an area long known as an agricultural Eden but only under vines since 1973, have demonstrated that high-quality, Bordeaux-style Merlot can be produced in this area's sandy soils and mild climate. Although several Long Island wines have earned recognition from wine critics, whether or not Long Island's wineries can survive solely on the merits of their wine, rather than tourist traffic, remains to be seen. It's too early to tell.

Argentina

As a wine-producing (and wine-loving) nation, Argentina enjoys many natural assets beneficial to wine production. Her vineyard regions are located in the western part of the country, scattered along the eastern foothills of the Andes range. These towering mountains shield the Argentine vineyards from Pacific rainstorms and yet provide them with a steady flow of water from their melting icecaps. Furthermore, the low humidity in this near-desert region prevents molds and other vineyard problems. Although it would be possible to cultivate a wide range of grape varieties in these conditions, it seems that the Argentine wine industry has adopted the Malbec grape variety of Southwest France as its own.

Brought to Argentina from France a century ago, the Malbec grape fares far better in Argentina's dry conditions than it ever did in its native Bordeaux, where it was especially susceptible to the mildew and rot encouraged by maritime humidity. In the hands of a great producer, Argentine Malbec is fruity and lush with a moderate backbone of tannin and acidity. Dr. Nicolás Catena, proprietor of the Botega Catena Zapata winery in Mendoza, produces some of the finest (and most expensive) versions of Argentine Malbec.

Other grape varieties that perform well or show future promise in Argentina are the usual international varieties Cabernet Sauvignon, Merlot, and Chardonnay. As in many other fine wine regions of the world, the Syrah grape is becoming significant in Argentina. However, if you want to try something a little farther from the mainstream, look for Argentine wine made from the Criolla grape, a low-end *vinifera* variety brought to Argentina hundreds of years ago. It is still quite popular in Argentina as an inexpensive, heavyweight white.

Chile

Chile, the 3,000-mile-long nation along the Pacific Coast of South America, is rapidly becoming one of the most important sources of inexpensive varietal wines in the world. California wines have steadily increased in price, to the point that a varietally correct $15 bottle of California Merlot or Cabernet Sauvignon is headed for the endangered species list. Chile is benefiting from this increase in Californian wine prices, producing generous quantities of California-style wines with forward and obvious fruit flavors.

Chile's wine regions are located in the approximate center of the country, just south of the capital city of Santiago, about halfway between the Pacific Ocean and the rugged Andes Mountains. Traveling south from Santiago, the region names most likely to appear on a wine label are:

Casablanca
Rapel
Maipo
Colchagua

However, like most New-World wines, Chilean wine is generally labeled primarily by grape variety. For the most part, the varieties echo those produced in neighboring Argentina, with one significant exception.

The Carménère variety was once cultivated extensively in Bordeaux, until it was overshadowed by other varieties and faded from use. At some point, it was brought to Chile and misidentified as Merlot. Until recently, it was labeled as such. Under close scrutiny by ampelographers (grapevine scientists), the Carménère grape was reidentified as distinct from Merlot, and many Chilean wineries now proudly bottle varietal Carménère.

Chile has a reputation as a source of inexpensive varietal wine, mostly reds. In order to establish itself as a source of fine wine, however, Chile must overcome this reputation. There has been a strong push toward quality winemaking in recent years, driven by significant investment from European and American wine producers. It remains to be seen if the American wine consumer will accept higher-priced, premium versions of Chilean wine.

South Africa

Fine wine has been produced in South Africa since the 1600s, when the region was colonized by the Dutch. However, because of the white South African government's policy of racial apartheid, South Africa was politically and economically ostracized for several decades during the wine boom and thus unable to reap its benefits. Although today it is politically acceptable to support the South African industry, there has not been any wholesale shift in consumer interest toward South African wine following its entry into the American market. This will undoubtedly change, because the wines of South Africa are rapidly improving.

Almost all of South Africa's vineyards are concentrated near the continent's southern tip, where the Indian Ocean meets the Atlantic. A cool current of Antarctic air and water refreshes the region with temperatures chillier than its warm latitude might suggest. Even so, until recently, most of South Africa's vineyards were planted in plains just a little too warm for fine wine production. Furthermore, many of the South African vineyard sites are in acidic soils that require costly amelioration. However, even with such disadvantages, there are some excellent South African wines on the market.

Pinotage is a red grape variety nearly unique to its South African birthplace. Also known by the name Hermitage, Pinotage is an attempted cross of Pinot Noir and Syrah.

However, some vines got mixed up, and the Cinsault of Southern France—far more pedestrian a grape than the intended Syrah—was successfully crossed with Pinot Noir instead. This new variety has been a success in South Africa, so much so that it has encouraged a few Californian vintners to give it a try. There have also been numerous successes with Cabernet Sauvignon, Merlot, and Syrah, known in South Africa as Shiraz.

Chenin Blanc (known in South Africa as "Steen") and Chardonnay grapes do well in this country, as does Sauvignon Blanc. The best of these wines are light and crisp, with contrasting elements of fruit and minerals.

The South African system of wine labeling requires that the geographic region of origin be specified on the wine labels. The most notable regions are:

Swartland
Stellenbosch
Paarl

As with American wines, South African wines must be comprised of at least 75 percent of a single grape variety in order to qualify for varietal labeling.

Australia

Australia has been making wine since soon after the first shipload of British settlers (and prisoners) arrived in 1788. Geographically isolated from the rest of the wine-producing world, Australia developed her own sophisticated winemaking technology largely independent of the techniques developed in Europe. This factor, along with a combination of intense sunshine and cool breezes, helps to make Australian wines unique. If California's famous wine regions are best characterized by their capacity for heat accumulation, Australia's regions are even more so. The sun-baked interior of Australia boasts only one brave wine producer; the rest of the Australian producers bask in the sun of more hospitable and grape-friendly regions clustered in the three southeastern states and one small area in the southwestern corner, in the state of Western Australia. Unlike almost all other wine regions on Earth, ripeness is never an issue in the vineyards of Australia, where the relentless sunshine reliably brings even high yields of grapes to absolute ripeness.

The hot and humid Hunter Valley, historically a source of Sémillon and Chardonnay, is close to the eastern coast, just north of Sydney in the state of New South Wales. It is perhaps Hunter Valley's proximity to Sydney, as much as the quality of its wines, that has brought the region such renown.

The Southeast . . .

Farther down the coast, the state of Victoria is a source of unusual dessert wines. The sweet Muscat and Tokay-based dessert wines of Rutherglen—known as "stickies" Down Under—are fortified blends of sweet wines from multiple vintages going back several decades. Elsewhere in Victoria is the cool Yarra Valley region, a rare source of Australian Pinot Noir, and the historic Great Western region.

The state of South Australia, perhaps Australia's most important wine-producing state, is home to several great wine regions. The Clare and Barossa Valleys are both famous for their Shiraz (Syrah)–based reds and, thanks to a strong

German heritage in the state, dry Rieslings characterized by the uniquely Australian hint of lime favor. The Padthaway region is a source of high-quality and affordable Chardonnay, and the very Australian-sounding Coonawarra region is considered Australia's finest source of Cabernet Sauvignon.

. . . And the Southwest

Thousands of miles away, on Western Australia's Indian Ocean coast, the small but rapidly improving Margaret River region is producing Cabernet Sauvignons and Chardonnays that compete with the finest wines of Australia's southeastern wineries.

New Zealand

The Southern Pacific nation of New Zealand, comprised of two main islands, has long been famous for her lamb wool, a world-class rugby team, and miles of unspoiled trout rivers. However, in the past decade, New Zealand has also become synonymous with distinctive and affordable wines made from the Sauvignon Blanc grape, a noble white variety that, even in its most brilliant manifestations, has never generated much excitement among the wine-buying public. Although it is not the most widely planted grape variety in New Zealand (that distinction belongs to Chardonnay), the Sauvignon Blanc grape appears to have found an ideal setting in New Zealand, particularly in the cool Marlborough region on the South Island. In the hands of skilled winemakers, Marlborough Sauvignon Blanc delivers an array of varietally correct aromas, ranging from grapefruit and gooseberry to funky animal scents. These aromas are accompanied by a racy acidic profile that makes this wine especially delicious to enjoy with dinner, rather than to drink by itself during cocktails.

The Rest of the World

This list of wine-producing countries is by no means comprehensive. There are well-made wines from many other regions that are beyond the scope of this book. If you're feeling adventurous, ask your local wine merchant about fine wines from Eastern Europe, or even Canada.

PART 3

Choosing and Serving Wine

CHAPTER 6

Tasting Wine

You walk into a wine shop, and the clerk asks if he can help you select a wine. You pause in thought, then turn in embarrassment and walk out the door. You know what kind of wine you like when you taste it, but you just don't know how to communicate that to the salesperson. Determining why you enjoy one wine over another and expressing yourself articulately are just a matter of practice and a few well-chosen words. In this chapter, you'll learn what makes wine good, the right way to taste wine, and a few things that could make normally good wine taste not-so-good.

What Makes Wine Good?

So, before you start tasting and buying wine, you need to know how to tell if wine is good. The "experts" out there have a near-monopoly in deciding what is good and what is not, but you can certainly decide for yourself what you like. As you learn more and more about wine, you will develop confidence in your own taste, and you will be able to taste a wine and know immediately if you like it or not. Furthermore, even if you don't exactly love a particular wine, you will be able to tell whether or not it is nonetheless a good, well-made wine. It might very well be that certain wines suit someone else's style, but not yours. To best illustrate the characteristics of quality wines, let's take a hypothetical look at a few "perfect" glasses of wine.

Wine #1: White Served at 45°–50°F

The first quality we notice is crystalline clarity—this wine is like a liquid diamond! The initial sniff fills our heads with aromas of wet stones, ripe peaches, and lime rinds. The first sip is so bracingly acidic that it is hard to comprehend fully. Then the second sip brings the flavors into sharp focus and reveals layer upon layer of fruit and mineral elements, along with bright, mouth-watering acidity perfectly balanced by a hint of sweetness. The flavors practically dance on your tongue and seem to last forever. This is what great Riesling from one of Germany's finest regions tastes like.

Wine #2: Red Served at 55°– 60°F

The glass of red, served about 10° or 15° warmer than the white, is its opposite in many ways. Unlike the crystal-clear white, the deep, purplish-black color of this wine is nearly opaque. Clearly, it is a densely flavored wine. Upon sniffing this wine, ripe aromas of blackberry and cassis greet your nose, along with a slight whiff of cedar and mint. This is a massive wine, and after just a small sip, your mouth is immediately flooded with these powerful fruit flavors, as well as a silky and detailed tannic structure, which provides just enough "grip" in your mouth.

There's no dancing here—this wine is too heavy and complex for that. Rather, you are carried away by the engaging array of heady textures, flavors, and aromas that remain in your mouth and memory long after swallowing each sip. This sort of heavenly red wine illustrates the greatness that Californian sunshine can coax from the Cabernet Sauvignon grape.

The Self-Fulfilling Prophesy of Perfection

Two wines, opposites in many ways, yet both are "perfect." What do they have in common? For starters, they were both meant to be great. Just as the Ford Taurus is a perfectly good car that will never win the Indianapolis 500, there are mass-produced but well-made wines on the market that are meant for nothing more than casual, everyday consumption. "Everyday" wine will never be mistaken for world-class wine. However, the two wines described here were meant to be great, and great care was taken to make them so.

Great wine is, in a way, a self-fulfilling prophesy. Knowing that his wine traditionally commands top price, a wine producer can justify a "spare no expense" approach in the vineyard and cellar. For instance, it is said that great wine is grown, not made, and no vineyard decision affects the quality of the final product as does the crop level, expressed in *tons per acre*. A typical Napa Valley Cabernet vineyard might be capable of ripening, say, five tons per acre, but a quality-conscious grower might decide to thin the crop so as to yield less than half that amount. By doing so, he is rewarded with exceptionally ripe grapes that yield a more richly textured and correspondingly pricier wine than if he had reaped and vinified the maximum crop.

Wooden aging barrels, once an absolute necessity for wine production, are now something of a luxury item. For most of the world's wine, the stainless-steel tank is a perfectly good place for a wine to repose before bottling, and yet the aroma gained from aging in French oak barrels is like expensive perfume. For many of the world's greatest wines, the unmistakable whiff of the French oak barrel is an integral component. These barrels cost about $700 each and thus add about $2.50 to the cost of producing a 750ml bottle of wine. Of course, wine barrels are used for several years, and their expense is thus spread over several vintages. But barrels are only new once, and many pricey wines—both red and white—spend part of their lives in new French oak.

Wine Wisdom

In its richest vintages, the famous dessert wine Château d'Yquem of Sauternes in Bordeaux is racked from its original new oak barrels into another round of new oak, thus justifying its proud boast of "200 percent new oak"—certainly a worthwhile expense for a $250 bottle.

Producers of less expensive wines employ various shortcuts to add the oak flavor, which has become, for many wine drinkers, an expected component of Chardonnay and other favorite varietal wines. Oak chips, when temporarily steeped in wine in a giant steel vat, can approximate to a somewhat acceptable degree the caramel-like flavor imparted by oak barrels, and this technique is used for many mass-market wines.

Great Grapes

Grape variety is of primary importance in the production of great wine; you cannot usually make a silk purse from a sow's ear, as the saying goes. While a profound wine might occasionally be produced from a pedestrian strain of grapes, the rare exceptions prove the rule: Great wine comes from great grapes. What makes certain grapes great? That's hard to say, except that centuries of experience have taught winemakers and wine lovers which grapes are responsible for the most prized wines.

For example, over the past several centuries, the Cabernet Sauvignon variety has proven to be one of the greatest of the red wine grapes. It is genetically endowed with a thick, flavorful skin and, therefore, requires considerable heat accumulation over the course of the growing season to attain full ripeness. Underripe Cabernet Sauvignon has an unpleasantly weedy, green flavor.

However, when grown to absolutely full ripeness on the sun- drenched hillsides of California or in the Gulf Stream–warmed Médoc in Bordeaux, the thick skin of the Cabernet Sauvignon grape reliably develops the unique chemical components that are responsible for Cabernet Sauvignon's signature array of flavors and aromas. Similarly, time and experience have shown winemakers in many parts of the world that the Riesling grape, when ripened under its own ideal conditions, yields luscious, crystal clear, nectar-like white wine with the unique fruit and mineral flavors that we have come to associate with the finest versions.

Other, inferior grapes grown under the same conditions as Cabernet Sauvignon and Riesling may indeed produce good wine, but will rarely equal wine made from these noblest of wine grapes. Of course, there are some great wines produced in wine regions unsuitable for Cabernet Sauvignon or Riesling. Chardonnay and Pinot Noir are arguably the co-equals of Riesling and Cabernet Sauvignon in the royal hierarchy of *Vitis vinifera*. Chardonnay is produced in a wide variety of wine regions around the world, including prime California acreage too warm for Riesling. And the early-ripening Pinot Noir becomes royalty-grade red wine in the continental climate of Burgundy, a region too cool for Cabernet Sauvignon.

Different wine grapes prefer different soils. Chardonnay, for instance, may grow in a wide variety of soils but seems to perform best in those with a chalk or limestone component, while Riesling seems quite happy in the slate-rich slopes of the Mosel valley. Among red wine grapes, Cabernet Sauvignon is known to perform well in well-drained soils of varied composition in many different parts of the world, while the more finicky Pinot Noir grape, like Chardonnay, seems to favor limestone-rich soils as in its native Burgundy.

Quantity over Quality?

Far away from the world's prized growing regions are the workhorse vineyards in which *quantity*, not *quality*, is of primary importance. The Languedoc region of Southern France was for many decades the source of nondescript country wine, mass-produced for daily consumption by France's working class. The Aramon grape, now thankfully banished to the history books, reliably yielded over twenty tons of grapes per acre in the Languedoc's relatively fertile loam. Here in America, the great Central Valley of California affords wine grapes the greatest heat accumulation in the Golden State, making it possible to ripen the most marketable varieties (if in name only) at obscenely high crop levels.

Lately, there is some good news from these volume-oriented outposts. France's Languedoc region is having great success with red Rhône varieties when crop levels are held in check. Likewise, Lodi, now a government-recognized quality wine-producing subregion of California's Central Valley, is now beginning to produce some remarkable versions of the heat-loving Zinfandel grape.

The Final Analysis

So, after all, what makes great wine great? In short, the world's greatest wines are usually those that are meant to be great, and recognized as such by the "experts" as well as the wine-buying public. In most (but not all) cases, great wines come from the best grape varieties, grown in the best soil in the world's great wine regions, and are produced by winemakers with the knowledge and desire to produce wines of such a caliber. Attention is paid to every detail, no matter how expensive. The fact that there are unpredictable exceptions to this axiom—surprising wines from unusual grapes or from lesser-known regions—is one of the things that keeps the wine world from becoming boring.

If you're like most people, the thought of savoring a truly "perfect" bottle of wine is an occasional luxury at best, and certainly not an experience to be replicated on a regular basis! Don't worry—there are thousands of wines made all over the world that are not "great" but are perfectly good wines to drink. Some of these, in fact, might even be terrific bargains. One of the keys to a lifetime of wine enjoyment is first learning what the great wines of the world taste like, and then finding inexpensive wines that remind you of them.

The Physiology of Taste

Taste is arguably subjective when art, fashion, or music is the subject of conversation. When wine is the subject, you will find that everyone may have different "tastes" in wine, but tasting wine has an objective component. For one thing, tasting wine (or anything!) involves not just taste but sight, smell, and touch. These fours senses send objective information to your brain, and this helps you evaluate, not merely appreciate, that glass in front of you. Whether you like what your brain is telling you, that is where subjectivity enters the picture. What you like is very much tied to your upbringing and cultural influences.

Whether you are evaluating wine or appreciating wine, setting is enormously important. That incredible bottle of Chianti you shared over a romantic dinner didn't measure up when you drank it alone in front of the TV, did it? Your taste is affected by your mood, by your health, and by your environment. Try to enjoy a floral Viognier when you have a cold or when you're in a smoke-filled room. It will be quite a challenge.

Sight

A wine's appearance influences your judgment. Color and clarity are the key things to look for. Is the color what you expected, or is it somehow off? Is clarity lacking because of any cloudiness that would indicate the wine is unfined? Are there any perfectly harmless tartrate crystals in that glass of white wine? In blind wine tastings, participants are sometimes given black, opaque glasses so they're not prejudiced by what the wine looks like, even by the color.

Color can tell you something about the age of wine. As white wines get older, they get darker. As red wines age, they lose color.

Smell

Your sense of smell is your most acute sense and is many times more sensitive than your sense of taste. You sense aromas either directly by inhaling through your nose, or indirectly through the nasal passage at the back of your mouth. Taste and smell are so linked that when you experience the generous dark fruit of a Cabernet Sauvignon, you are actually tasting aromas of that dark fruit. Speaking of fruit, don't be surprised if you think of blackberries as you smell your Cab. Wine is made up of hundreds of chemical compounds, many of which are similar—or identical—to those in fruits, vegetables, flowers, herbs, and spices. The winemaker did not add essence of blackberry to that wine; your brain is simply picking up one of those compounds.

Taste

In contrast to the multitude of aromas the nose can identify, the tongue recognizes only four basic tastes: sweetness, saltiness, acidity, and bitterness, and some might say umami. Saltiness doesn't come into play when tasting wine, but the others are critical. The tongue does not register these four or five tastes at distinct sites as was previously thought. It has been proven that taste occurs everywhere on the tongue.

Sweetness and acidity are the yin and yang of the wine-tasting world. They balance each other. Think of lemonade. Lemon juice on its own is a mouth-puckering experience. The more sugar you add to the juice, the less you notice the acidity.

When tasting wine, never judge a wine on the first sip. Your mouth must first adjust to the alcohol and acidity before it can more accurately convey that wine's other attributes. It's also better to taste before lunch or dinner, not after. Your senses heighten as you get hungry.

Bitterness plays a role in winetasting as well. Red wine tannin, while having more of a tactile nature than a taste, can give you the impression of bitterness.

Touch

Wines have texture that you can feel in your mouth. A wine can be thin—like water. Or it can be full—like cream. That's what a wine's "body" is all about. "Full-bodied" and "light-bodied" are not subjective judgments; they are descriptions.

Your mouth distinguishes other sensations as well. Tannins, the elements responsible for a wine's ability to age, have an astringent, mouth-drying effect very much like the impression you get when you drink oversteeped tea. The alcohol in the wine will give you a hot feeling at the back of your throat and on the roof of your mouth.

Your perception of a wine's body—its texture and fullness—is due mostly to the amount of alcohol in the wine. The more potent a wine is, the more full-bodied it will seem. For example, a big Zinfandel with 16 percent alcohol content will have more body than a Riesling with 9 percent.

Right and Wrong Ways to Taste

There's nothing wrong with simply picking up your glass of wine and taking a swig. If you really want to understand the wine while you're enjoying it, you might want to employ techniques used by wine-industry professionals.

Swirling

After examining the color and clarity, give the wine a swirl. If you are afraid of ruining your brand new polo shirt, set the glass on a smooth surface, grasp the stem near the base, and move the glass in circles. As the wine rotates, aromas intensify and tannins soften ever so slightly. Before the aromas escape and are lost, stick your nose right into the glass. Don't just sniff; rather, inhale deeply.

Once is rarely enough. Swirl the wine again and inhale. You can't possibly take in all the aroma nuances at once. Close your eyes. What scents are you detecting? You may smell something new each time.

Swishing and Slurping

After experiencing the wine's aromas, it's time to taste. Wine pros savor the moment. Take a generous sip and give it time to linger in your mouth. Better yet, swish the wine around in your mouth. Touch every surface of your tongue with wine. Hit every taste receptor. Quickly swallowing a small sip barely does the wine justice. If you are tasting a tart, herbal Sauvignon Blanc, that quick sip will probably just leave the impression of tartness and little else.

Once you've mastered swishing, try slurping. Purse your lips and draw in some air across the wine on your tongue. It's called slurping because that's the sound this technique makes. Slurping intensely aerates the wine, making it easier for aroma compounds to waft up your rear nasal passage and reach the olfactory bulb that allows your brain to make sense of those aromas. Depending on the number of wines you plan to sample, you may want to spit out the wine you just evaluated. Alcohol dulls the senses over time, so if learning is your goal, it's perfectly fine to spit.

Mastering the Lingo

When wine lovers get excited about a new wine find, they want to share the experience. The only trouble is that words are often so inadequate. Talking about wine has become intimidating, since many terms seem mysterious and pretentious. A place to start is to compare your glass of Merlot to things that are familiar to you, such as your aunt's famous cherry pie. For those wine lovers who may not have sampled your aunt's pie, here are some terms that every wine lover should be familiar with.

- **Dry**—It's the opposite of sweet. When all the sugar in the grape juice has been converted to alcohol and carbon dioxide, the wine is said to be bone dry. There is a continuum, however, between really sweet and really dry. If enough residual sugar remains to give the wine a slight sweetness, the wine is off-dry.
- **Balance**—None of the wine's components is out of whack. The acid, alcohol, fruit, and tannins all work together so that one doesn't stand apart from the rest.
- **Finish**—A wine's aftertaste, or the flavor or aroma that lingers after you've swallowed the wine, is referred to as

its finish. If it has one, it's considered a good thing and the longer the better. A "long finish" is a real compliment.

- **Complex**—Layers and nuances of flavor make a wine complex. A complex wine will continue to reveal itself as you sip it. This multidimensional quality is often achieved with aging. A complex wine is also said to have depth.
- **Crisp**—A wine with good acidity and no excessive sweetness is crisp. Think of an apple. The wine is relatively high in acidity, but the acidity doesn't overwhelm the other components.

In general, some of the aromas you'll be able to discern from white wines are melon, apple, pineapple, pear, citrus, vanilla, caramel, flowers, herbs, grass, minerals, olives, and butterscotch. Some flavors and aromas from red wines are berries, cedar, currants, plums, cherries, blackberries, flowers, earth, wood, smoke, chocolate, tobacco, leather, and coffee.

Wine Wisdom

Many people confuse sweetness and fruitiness. They can't be blamed. Very often, wine labels describe sweet wine as fruity. If you have some doubt about what you're tasting, take a sip of the wine while holding your nose. If the wine is sweet, you'll taste its sweetness on your tongue—instead of sensing the aroma of the fruit.

Recognizing "Flaws"

Wine flaws are not necessarily the result of bad winemaking. Wines can be defective if they have been improperly handled or stored. That said, the presence of a wine flaw or defect does not automatically make the wine bad and worthy only of cooking. The key is knowing how much is too much. Certain characteristics that make a wine flawed can actually, in small amounts, be considered by some people to be a plus. It could be considered similar to adding garlic to food: A little bit enhances the dish, but too much ruins it. Here are common culprits behind most wine faults.

Corks

Your wine smells of damp cardboard or musty basement. Whether the odor is pronounced or just slightly dank, it came from a cork tainted with a chemical compound called TCA. When the wine is damaged in this way, it's said to be corked. By industry estimates, 3–5 percent of all wines are corked. Cork processing improvements have been made to eliminate TCA, but many wineries are so fed up they are resorting to closures such as screw tops and synthetic corks as permanent remedies. Cork taint never enhances a wine.

Oxygen

The wine tastes dull, cooked, or a little Sherry-like. A white wine has an off color—brownish or very dark yellow. These are all indications that the wine has been exposed to excessive oxygen. It could have happened while the wine was being made or when it was being stored. If wines are stored upright for long periods instead of on their sides, the cork can dry out and let air into the bottle.

Perhaps your wine smells like vinegar or nail polish remover. This is an extreme case traceable to a bacterium called acetobacter and oxygen. Acetobacter is everywhere— on grape skins, winery walls, and barrels. By itself, it has no aroma or flavor, but when it meets oxygen in winemaking, it first produces the compound ethyl acetate (nail polish remover) before completely reducing the wine to acetic acid (the vinegar aroma). The term "volatile acidity" (VA) accounts for these two conditions, although once a wine reaches the level of acetic acid, it's considered oxidized. Many wine connoisseurs enjoy low levels of ethyl acetate.

Yeast

Your wine smells like a barnyard or Band-Aids. It may be the result of a yeast called Brettanomyces—brett, for short. Brett grows on grapes and in wineries and is difficult to eradicate. Winemakers use special filters to help reduce its growth. Some wine drinkers enjoy a low level of brett, maintaining that it adds complexity to the wine's aroma, but too much completely spoils the wine.

Sulfur Dioxide

Your wine smells like a struck match. Winemakers add sulfur dioxide to preserve the wine, but in excess it ruins the wine. Cheap white wines are most likely to have sulfur problems.

Heat

The wine is brown, and it smells like it's been cooked. In Madeira, this is a plus and part of the wine's essential character. Elsewhere, it's a flaw, and the term "maderized" will be used. The wine has likely experienced severe fluctuations of temperature in a short period of time or been stored in extreme heat. If the cork is protruding slightly from an unopened bottle, the wine could be maderized.

CHAPTER 7

Navigating the Restaurant Wine List

If choosing the right wine for dinner at home is stressful, ordering the right wine from a restaurant's wine list can be downright intimidating. The wine selections available in restaurants often include older vintages, limited-production wines, and other hard-to-find treasures. Wine is also considerably more expensive in restaurants than in wine stores.

Buying Wine in a Restaurant

Once you become familiar with various types of wine and figure out what kinds you really like, there is not that much more to know about buying wine in a restaurant . . . except that it costs a lot more. The more you learn about wine, the more painfully aware you become of the prices of wine in restaurants. If you enjoy going to restaurants and want to enjoy wine when you are there, consider the following:

1. **Food is often marked up more than wine:** Good restaurants usually mark up food about three and a

half times. In other words, a $20 entree probably costs the restaurant about $6 to prepare. While some restaurants mark up their wine just as much as their food, most restaurants charge around double their wholesale cost for mid-priced wines. A restaurant adds expertise and convenience when preparing the raw ingredients of your entree. Insist on the same with your wine— proper serving temperature (see Chapter 6), sparkling clean and appropriate glassware, and attentive service are all essential to a pleasurable wine-drinking experience in restaurants.

2. **If nobody bought wine, there would be fewer restaurants:** Most restaurants need wine sales to survive. If you enjoy dining at a particular restaurant, your wine purchases will help to keep it there.

3. **You can send it back . . . within reason:** If a wine has gone bad or suffers from cork spoilage, any restaurant should gladly take it back. If a wine steward or waiter has enthusiastically recommended a wine and you don't like it, you should also be allowed to return it.

But if you simply don't like a wine, step back a bit. Do others at your table agree? Have you tasted it without food? If so, taste it with a well-chewed piece of bread in your mouth. Wine is meant to be tasted with food. Might it need to breathe? If you aren't sure, ask the waiter to pour some wine into a glass, and let it breathe for a few minutes. If you still just don't like it, a good restaurant will probably try to keep you happy, especially if you are a regular customer. It is best not to make a habit of this practice, however.

By the way, most wines sent back in restaurants go back to the supplier, thus relieving the restaurant of the cost. The exception to this is older wine.

Older Wine

Let's say you're in a restaurant and you order a twenty-year-old Bordeaux. This wine might have been in the restaurant's cellar for fifteen years. At $100 a bottle, you have a right to expect good, solid wine. However, can you send it back if, while showing no flaws, it fails to live up to your expectations? Probably, but you should consider that the price of older wine often reflects its scarcity rather than its intrinsic value. You pay a premium for the opportunity to enjoy wine on your twentieth anniversary from, say, the year of your marriage. So be thoughtful about returning such wines. In this case, the restaurant will probably have to eat the cost of the bottle. (Depending on when they bought it, this might be a surprisingly small amount of money.)

Wine by the Glass Is Often Very Expensive

In restaurants, the markup on bottles of wine is far less than the markup on mixed drinks. Because many customers now order a glass of wine in place of that initial cocktail, smart restaurant operators ensure that they make the same money on that drink and mark up wine by the glass accordingly. Premium wine by the glass is a better value, a category in which the markup is more in line with the wine program than with the martini program. These premium wines by the glass are a convenient service for those who can't agree on a bottle or don't want to drink that much.

Making a Selection

This is the fun part! Ordering a bottle with which you are familiar is the safest option; however, many of California's finest treasures are available only to fine restaurants. You might have read glowing reviews of such wines, only to find them impossible to purchase from a wine merchant. It follows that you won't get after-the-fact sticker shock by spotting such a gem on a retail shelf for far less than the restaurant's price.

Restaurant lists are also likely to offer older vintages of special reds worthy of cellaring. It makes no financial sense for a retail store to age wine, but wines from older vintages—perhaps a "vertical" (multiple vintages) of a particular producer—can draw wine buffs to a restaurant. And so you might order a special bottle that is unavailable anywhere else, or a mature red from an old vintage . . . or just an inexpensive bottle to accompany your meal.

Wine Wisdom

Everyone who buys wine develops a price point in their mind beyond which they are not comfortable, for fear that they will not appreciate a wine's value. The more you learn about wine, the more this price point will go up.

A table of four might have ordered fish, pasta, chicken, and steak, and finding the "perfect wine" might be impossible. You don't need to. Most restaurants with well-managed wine programs offer half-bottles, and a table of four can easily enjoy two different wines at the same time.

Finally, a restaurant wine program is only as good as its service, and a professional wine steward should be on the staff in a well-run establishment. It is his or her job to know something about every wine on the list, and to be able to describe it to you accurately. The days of the snooty, intimidating, and condescending wine steward are thankfully over, now that wine has become a more integral part of our culture. Accordingly, you should be able to rely on the wine steward's advice if you have any questions. Offering the wine steward a small taste of your wine is an excellent way to show your gratitude while contributing to his or her continuing education.

Enjoying Wine with Your Dinner

Just as at home, in a restaurant you have some control over the enjoyment of your wine. Is this white too cold? Let it warm up on the table and in the glass, and taste the hidden flavors as they emerge. Is the red too warm? Your server should cool it for you in ice water for five minutes or so. Your server should also be pouring the wine for you—in proper glassware, never more than half full—though it is okay to pour it yourself. Don't drink it all before the food arrives (unless you're planning to buy another bottle, of course).

The Wine Ritual

In restaurants, there is a certain ritual of procedure that takes place when wine is served. You order the wine, and you are shown the label. Is it the right year? If you ordered a "reserve," make sure it is not a lesser bottling from the same producer. So far, so good. Tell the server to keep the cork, unless you collect corks; it is of no use to you once you have verified that it hasn't rotted during its years in the bottle. Do taste the wine while the server is there. Any problem should be addressed immediately. Your server should then pour wine for everyone at the table.

Can You Bring Your Own Bottle (BYOB)?

This is an ongoing debate between some (but not all) restaurant owners and serious wine collectors. The restaurateurs argue that selling wine for a profit is an essential part of their business, just as selling food is. If they allow customers to bring in their own wine, they reason, they lose out on profits. Why not just let customers bring their own food as well? The pro-BYOB faction, meanwhile, argues that restaurant wine prices are outrageously high, and that many wine connoisseurs would fill the restaurants' empty seats if they were permitted to bring their cellar treasures to enjoy with a well-prepared restaurant meal.

A compromise position is the "corkage fee," a price added to the dinner bill of those customers who bring their own wine. This fee helps to offset the lost profit on a wine sale and the costs of maintaining glassware. Corkage fees of $10 or even $20 are reasonable. Ironically, there are stories of some fancy restaurants charging $100 or more, which is as predatory as many of the wine list prices that inspire customers to bring their own bottles in the first place.

Here are some points of BYOB etiquette:

- Always ask ahead of time if BYOB is allowed. (It is actually illegal in some states.) Know the corkage fee beforehand as well.

- It is rude to bring a bottle that is already on the restaurant's wine list. If you're going to BYOB, bring something special.
- Remember that it costs the waiter a wine tip when you bring your own.
- Offer the wine steward a taste of your special wine—this just might get your corkage fee waived.
- Remember that restaurants are not government-subsidized picnic areas for your wine enjoyment. They are in business to make money, and they are doing you a favor when they let you BYOB.

The Bottom Line

Unless you care to cook elaborate meals for yourself and your guests on a regular basis, paying restaurant prices for wine is unavoidable. When ordering wine in a restaurant, we recommend taking the opportunity to enjoy special wines that are otherwise unavailable to you. Knowledge is power—having some idea of what "restaurant only" wines actually cost the restaurant is obviously useful and can often be inferred from published ratings.

CHAPTER 8

Wine and Food

A century ago, everyone just drank their local wine and didn't fret about the "perfect match" for a meal. Then, as diners began demanding more from their gastronomical experiences, a set of "rules" developed governing the pairing of food and wine. The classic is red wine with meat and white wine with fish, but as chefs became more inventive, the number of rules grew. The truth is food and wine pairing is somewhat subjective, but there are certain principles that can guide you.

The Dynamics of Food and Wine

Food and wine are like a pair of ballroom dancers. Each one affects the performance of the partner. Sometimes they're slightly out of step, but sometimes their footwork meshes seamlessly. On occasion, they move as one and transform a simple dance into a moment of magic. Even on those rare occasions when both partners seem to have two left feet, the experience was still probably worth it.

Food and wine, whatever their individual personalities, influence the way each other tastes. A particular food can exaggerate or diminish the flavor of a wine. A certain wine can overwhelm a certain dish.

Wine As a Condiment

Cooks who are passionate about wine often choose the wine first and match the food to it. The general practice, however, is to start with the food and add the wine later. When the time comes to pick the wine, it helps to think of the wine as a condiment. The most basic step in matching wine and food is to assess their common flavors and textures.

Fine-dining restaurants exert a great deal of effort in this department. Many menus will suggest wines for each course, and these recommendations are not made at the whim of the chef. Before anything gets into print, the chef, the sommelier, and sometimes the wait staff all taste-test various combinations. They might taste Hermitage and Bordeaux with the rosemary-crusted rack of lamb or Sancerre and Chablis with the seared scallops tossed in butter and ginger.

They compare and discuss, and often disagree, but they save time by knowing that some food textures (creamy, oily, crunchy) simply will not complement certain wine textures (crisp, astringent, viscous).

Too Many Variables

It used to be you could order a steak and French fries and a glass of Cabernet. Things became more complicated with the advent of fusion food, with dozens of ingredients in one preparation.

Ingredients are not the only things influencing the flavors of a dish; cooking processes do as well. You can have your food baked, boiled, broiled, grilled, poached, sautéed, fried, marinated, pasteurized, tenderized, and liquefied. You would not suggest the same wine with baked chicken as you would for barbecued chicken.

Wine can be even more complicated, with thousands of grapes, endless blending combinations, a dry-to-sweet continuum, oak-aging variables, and numerous alcohol ranges, to name a few. It's enough to make you want to throw your hands up in defeat and just order a beer. Rest assured that only a handful of food and wine pairings will actually ruin your meal. What follows is simply to help you get the most out of your dining experience, whether at home or at a restaurant.

Matching Likes to Likes

The following principles won't tell you exactly what to order on your next night out, but they'll help you understand why some foods and some wines make compatible partners. The principles are based on the four tastes that the tongue can discern—sweet, sour, salty, and bitter—and the idea is to match similar tastes in both the food and the wine.

A Sour Taste in Your Mouth

Foods that have a sour component are good matches for wines that are high in acid. A salad with a vinaigrette dressing and a fish fillet squirted with lemon both cry out for a high-acid wine. Acid is the bridge connecting the wine and the food. Compare the sensation of squeezing some lemon juice onto your tongue with that of sipping a Sauvignon Blanc. Your mouth will pucker. That's the acidity. (Notice here that you're not matching the wine to the fish fillet itself or to the lettuce in the salad. You're taking into consideration the preparation.) Tomatoes, onions, green peppers, and green apples are examples of other high-acid foods.

Savvy Sipping

Acidity is much more important in the taste and structure of white wines than red wines. Red wines do have acidity, although in many of them the bitterness of tannins influences your perception of that acidity. White wines have minimal tannins, so acidity plays a greater role.

Potential high-acid wine partners include Sauvignon Blanc and the northern French whites of Sancerre, Pouilly-Fumé, Vouvray, and Chablis. The wines of Alsace and Germany generally have high acidity. The acids in reds are often masked by the tannins, but safe bets are Italian reds. (Why do you think Italian wines go so perfectly with tomato-based pasta sauces?) The following whites are listed from low acid levels to high acid levels:

- Gewürztraminer (low)
- California Chardonnay (low to medium)
- Pinot Gris/Pinot Grigio (medium)
- Champagne (medium to high)
- Chablis (high)
- Chenin Blanc (high)
- Sancerre/Sauvignon Blanc (high)
- German Riesling (high)

Sweet Thing

The sweeter the food, the less sweet and more dull a wine will taste. If you pair a slice of roast pork with a glass of off-dry Chenin Blanc, the sweetness of the wine will be obvious. Top your pork with a heaping spoonful of pineapple glaze and your glass of wine will taste positively dry. When you get to dessert, the rule of thumb is to drink a wine that's sweeter than your food. Even a moderately sweet wine can taste thin, unpleasantly dry, and even sour when you pair it with a sugar blockbuster. Some suggested pairings:

- Pear tart and Sauternes
- New York cheesecake and Muscat
- Bread pudding and late-harvest Riesling
- Tiramisu and Port
- Dark chocolate mousse and Banyuls

Vino Veritas

Is there a way to tell how sweet or dry a wine is before you buy it? Look at the size of the bottle. Most dry wines are packaged in 750 ml bottles. Historically, dessert wines come in 375 ml half-bottles.

Don't Be Bitter

Bitterness in wine is caused by tannins, compounds that enter the wine from the skins of the grape submerged in the fermentation tank with the grape juice. Oak barrels also impart tannins, but skins are the main source. Tannins only apply to red wines. When you eat food with a hint of bitterness (olives, bok choy, or sauerkraut) and drink a wine with some bitterness, the bitterness and accompanying astringency is magnified. So be careful pairing Cabernet Sauvignon with German food! The following red wines are listed from low to high tannin levels:

- Beaujolais (low)
- Pinot Noir (low)
- Sangiovese (medium)
- Merlot (medium)
- Zinfandel (medium to high)
- Syrah/Shiraz (high)
- Cabernet Sauvignon (high)

Salt of the Earth

There are no salty wines, but there are plenty of salty foods: ham, smoked salmon, oysters, and teriyaki beef. The best way to cut salt is with high-acid wines. The salt in the food can also minimize the tartness of the wine and amplify the fruit.

More Than Taste

Once you understand how the taste of food and the taste of wine influence each other, the next piece to consider is how weight or body affects a food and wine match. Wine, like food, has power. Compare a Sancerre with a Napa Valley Cabernet Sauvignon. The latter has more muscle. The Sancerre would never hold up to a fiery French pepper steak the way the Cabernet would.

Alcohol is one of the contributors to a wine's sense of body and weight. The higher the alcohol, the greater the body or heavier the weight. So, even before tasting the wine, you can gauge its body by its alcohol content. A fuller-bodied wine will generally have more than 13 percent alcohol. Lighter-bodied wines typically are under 13 percent alcohol.

Cutting the Fat

A common impression is that tannic wines will "cut the fat." This is true, but not in the sense that it cuts the fat content of your 10-ounce filet mignon. Tannins are attracted to fatty proteins. As you chew your steak, your mouth is left with a coating of those fatty proteins. When you sip your glass of Cabernet, the tannin molecules attach themselves to the protein molecules—taking them along for the ride when you swallow. Not only is the Cabernet well matched in terms of weight, the ability of the steak to rob the wine of its tannins really brings out the rich, dark fruit of the wine.

Spice Up Your Life!

When you walk on the fiery side with dishes from Thailand, Mexico, or India, choosing a wine can be tough. Your usual dry favorites somehow make the exciting heat of the food downright painful. Tannins and alcohol are to blame. However, this does not mean you have to put wine aside altogether and reach for a glass of milk.

Wine Wisdom

It's not foolproof, but one way to estimate a wine's tannin level is by its color. The lighter it is, the less tannin the wine is likely to have. It stands to reason: The longer the skins stay in contact with the clear grape juice during fermentation, the more color and tannins they impart.

A sweeter, lower-alcohol wine is a much more soothing match for spicy foods. Try an off-dry Riesling or Gewürztraminer. If you only like red wine, Pinot Noir and Beaujolais are definite candidates with their lower alcohol and tannin levels.

Good Wine and Food Matches

If you're still stumped about the right wine to serve with the food you prepare at your next dinner party, or you draw a blank every time you need to decide on an appropriate wine to drink with your meal at a restaurant, read on.

Red Meat Dishes	
Food	**Wine**
Chili con carne	Beaujolais (an easy-drinking red); Zinfandel (a red to stand up to your chili)
Grilled steak	Cabernet Sauvignon (an ultimate match); Shiraz/Syrah (a good choice at a better price)
Hamburger	Any red wine you like that is inexpensive
Roast beef	Pinot Noir and Merlot (softer reds than for your grilled steak). If you are wild about Cabernet Sauvignon, then have a Cabernet from Bordeaux
Steak au poivre (steak with black peppercorn sauce)	BIG REDS: Zinfandel from California and Rhône reds are perfect
Tenderloin	Same as for roast beef: Pinot Noir and Merlot are the good choices

Poultry Dishes

Food	Wine
Chicken (roasted)	Almost any wine you like—this is a very versatile dish
Chicken (highly seasoned)	Chenin Blanc, Riesling, or other unoaked white
Turkey	Rosé, sweet or dry; rich and heavy whites
Duck and goose	Pinot Blanc or Viognier among whites and Merlot or Rhônes among reds
Game Birds	Pinot Noir

Other Meat Dishes

Food	Wine
Ham	Rosé; fruity Pinot Noir; Pinot Gris; Gewürztraminer
Lamb (simple)	Cabernet (especially from Bordeaux); red Rioja from Spain
Lamb (with herbs and garlic)	Cabernet Sauvignon; Spanish reds; Rhônes
Pork	A light Italian or Spanish red; Viognier, Pinot Gris, Gewürztraminer, or some other rich white
Sausage	Gewürztraminer or a rustic red
Veal	Richer whites, such as Chardonnay; light reds
Venison	A big red wine: Cabernet, Nebbiolo, Syrah, or Zinfandel will do well

The Book of Wine

Seafood Dishes

Food	Wine
Anything with a cream sauce	White Burgundy (clean, crisp Chardonnay)
Lobster	Champagne; dry Riesling; white Burgundy
Oysters	Muscadet, a French white, is ideal with oysters; Chablis (dry French Chardonnay)
Salmon	Sauvignon Blanc
Shrimp	Light and dry white wine
Swordfish	Light to medium white wines of all sorts
Tuna	This fish is versatile like chicken; anything but a big red is okay; a light red is probably the ideal match
White fish (sole, for instance)	Sauvignon Blanc; light Chardonnay

Pasta Dishes

Food	Wine
Red sauce	Barbera; Chianti or another Sangiovese-based red
Vegetables	Grüner Veltliner, Sauvignon Blanc, or other crisp whites
White sauce	Pinot Grigio

Some General Food-Wine Categories

Category	Characteristics	Examples
Fish Whites	Crisp, light, and acidic	Muscadet, Macon, Pinot Grigio, Sauvignon Blanc
Turkey Whites	Rich and heavy whites to accompany holiday meals	Viognier, Pinot Gris, Gewürztraminer
Fish Reds	Light and acidic reds with little tannin	Sangiovese, lighter Barbera, lighter reds, lighter Merlot, Burgundy, and other Pinot Noir
Pepper steak Reds	Big, bold reds that stand up to strongly flavored dishes	Châteauneuf-du-Pape, Cabernet Sauvignon, Malbec, Syrah/Shiraz

Warning: Bad Matches Ahead

Some foods are difficult to match with wine—not impossible, but problematic. Here are a few of the less-than-ideal candidates for wine partnerships:

- Artichokes
- Asparagus
- Chocolate
- Olives
- Spinach

When "difficult" foods are part of the menu, there's a way to get around the food-wine clash (assuming the difficult partner isn't the only food on the plate): Take a bite of something neutral, such as rice or bread, between bites and sips. Some difficult foods can be made less difficult with the addition of salt or a squirt of lemon, but they might still impart a metallic taste or blast of bitterness when you bring them together with your favorite wine.

Enemies of Food

On occasion, the wine is the difficult partner. There are some elements in wine that, when in full force, just don't taste good with food. Alcohol is one of them. It's a defining part of wine, but highly alcoholic wines are better drunk by themselves. More often than not, lower-alcohol wines are more flexible with foods.

Oak can be another problem. The toasty or vanilla flavor it adds is pleasant and popular, but is hardly a friend of food. These wines might be best enjoyed during the cocktail hour before you sit down to dinner.

Entertaining with Wine

Now that you know how (and how not!) to pair your favorite wines with your favorite foods, let's take a look at what you need to keep in mind while serving wine to guests. How much do you need for a large group? How much should you spend for a small dinner party? Read on.

Wine for Entertaining a Crowd

Let's say 50 (or 250) of your friends or relatives are getting together for an informal dinner or even a cocktail party with hors d'oeuvres and wine. Because of your interest in wine, you've been put in charge of getting the wine for the event . . . it sounds daunting, but it is really quite simple.

They Call Them "Crowd Pleasers" for a Reason

A large gathering of guests who probably don't know each other very well is not a good place to show off your wine expertise. Save the obscure Alsace Gewürztraminer and the puckery Portuguese red for your next wine tasting with friends, and stick to wines with broad appeal—crowd pleasers—for big events. Chardonnay and Merlot from California (or even Washington State) conform to most people's idea of a decent glass of wine, but you needn't confine yourself to just these two wines. For instance, an Italian-themed gathering would probably appreciate good varietal Sangiovese and Pinot Grigio. No matter what type of party you're having, you would always do well to have some White Zinfandel on hand in addition to your dry red and white choices. Make sure to choose a red and a white that are similarly priced so that one group or the other doesn't feel slighted. Buying a red and a white from the same producer that are the same price ("line priced" in retail-speak) lends some uniformity to an event.

Establish a Budget and Calculate Your Needs

Choosing the wines is a simple matter once you know how much you are authorized to spend. Try to deal with a store that will not only give you a significant quantity discount but will also take back for credit any unopened bottles! This will take the guesswork out of your purchase. Just make sure that overenthusiastic servers or helpers don't open more bottles than necessary. You can't do much with a box of half-empty bottles the next day. Figure on at least half a (750ml) bottle per person, divided evenly between red and white. Remember, as long as the store will take back the extras, you can aim high.

You Need Glasses!

If you're throwing a big party, spend a little money and rent some decent wine glasses, because fancy wine in a plastic cup doesn't usually taste as good as slightly less expensive wine in a real wine glass. Wine glasses and champagne "flutes" cost about thirty cents each to rent; therefore, assuming each glass is refilled once, you could pay for the glassware rental by downgrading the cost of the wine you're serving by only seventy-five cents per bottle.

Ice Is Nice

Nobody has ever had too much ice for a party. Most household refrigerators aren't powerful enough to chill a lot of wine on short notice, and ice—lots of it—is the best way to chill large quantities of beverages for a party. You can spend too much money on those little two-gallon bags of ice. It would be great if you are friendly enough with your favorite restaurant that you could arrange in advance to pick up a picnic cooler or two full of ice from them the morning of your party. Alternatively, a brand-new garbage can with a plastic bag liner works well enough (as long as nobody throws garbage in it!).

Wine for Small Dinner Parties

A small dinner party of eight to twelve people is a perfect way to show off your cooking skills—and your ability to match interesting wines with each course.

Keep It Simple

Your house is not a restaurant with the space and equipment to put out hundreds of plates of food in one night, so try to keep the menu to a manageable size. Likewise, your guests are coming to enjoy each other's company as well as the food and wine—and then drive home safely. Keeping the number of different wines to no more than three is a good idea.

Plan Your Lineup

A lineup of three dinner party wines might go like this:

- Sparkling wine (with hors d'oeuvres)
- White wine (with a light first course)
- Red (with the main course)

If you are not having a "light first course" but instead are jumping right to the main course, eliminating one wine affords you the opportunity to offer an interesting dessert wine later on, something even many wine lovers rarely get to try. Of course, a perfectly good dinner party can certainly be built around fewer than three wines.

No matter how many wines you serve, remember that you will need the right glassware for each wine. Here's a quick rundown of glassware:

- **White wine glasses** have a shape that looks a lot like a tulip. These all-purpose glasses can also be used to serve sparkling or red wine. Just remember that you should never serve white wine in a red wine glass.
- **Red wine glasses** are usually larger than their white counterparts. They have a rounder bowl, which enhances the wine's aroma because it allows for more air contact.
- **Flutes** are used to serve sparkling wines or champagne. These tall, thin glasses work best to bring out the delicate scent and effervescence of the wine. (Dessert wine glasses are similar in shape to flutes.)
- **Dessert glasses** are like smaller white wine glasses.

Remember that any style of wine glass should always be held by the stem. Aesthetically speaking, this keeps fingerprints off of the glass, but, more importantly, it also prevents the wine from heating up too much. If you're in need of a good all-purpose wine glass, look for one that holds at least 10 ounces and curves in at the top. This helps the wine to hold its scent.

Make It Interesting
"Crowd pleasers" are appropriate for a large gathering, but a small dinner party calls for less recognized wines with some pizzazz. For example, serving a highly rated new re-

lease of a special wine would give your guests a fun way to gauge their tastes against that of a professional reviewer, and wine from an unusual grape variety or a lesser-known producer will make the whole experience more interesting and memorable.

Be Flexible
In spite of all the thought you might put into matching the right wines with each course, one or more of your guests might prefer to drink only the white (or only the red) throughout the meal. No problem—just make sure you have enough of each wine to allow for this option.

Wine for Last Minute Guests

If you ever find yourself frantically trying to put together a last-minute dinner for your wine-savvy son and his new girlfriend whom you haven't yet met, there is no time to consult your list of food and wine pairing rules. When situations such as these occur, here are some fast and easy ways to make your food and wine experience more enjoyable.

Back to the Home Country

If your meal has German, Italian, French, or Spanish connections, the simple wine solution comes from the home country. Europeans have rarely made a big deal about matching food and wine. They just cooked the way they wanted and made wines that went well with their foods. Globalization of wine notwithstanding, Europeans still produce wines that taste good with their traditional fare.

If paella is on the menu, a red Rioja will be the best choice. Schnitzel and spaetzle? German Riesling. Osso buco screams for Barolo, and a Côtes du Rhône would nicely complement your pot-au-feu.

Instantly Food-Friendly Wines

Of course, the system breaks down when the ethnic region of choice has no long history of winemaking. Chinese, Thai, Cuban, and Indian cuisines come to mind immediately. There is still hope, however. Some wines are just naturally friendly. They make ideal dining partners no matter what you eat. You can choose one of them in any situation with the confidence that it will make a good match:

1. Champagne or sparkling wine
2. Riesling, if you're in the mood for white
3. Pinot Noir, if you feel like a red

Wine Wisdom

If the dish you're serving is overly salty and you can't repair the food somehow, the wine can come to the rescue. Serve a wine on the sweeter side—perhaps an off-dry Riesling or Muscat. It will make the food taste less salty.

"House Wine" for Everyday Sipping

If you are one of the growing number of Americans who enjoy a glass or two of wine every night with dinner, you might want to consider choosing a "house wine" to purchase in quantity and keep on hand. This way, you'll save both money and time.

Narrow Your Search

A good reason for buying a mixed case (besides saving 15 percent) is that it gives you a chance to try different wines in your style and price range before you commit to a particular bottling. A knowledgeable wine merchant should gladly help you assemble some choices. You might spend more on "house wine," you might spend less, but there are a great number of choices, both red and white, available for around $10 . . . before your case discount!

If you like light, crisp whites, the best bargains in that category usually come from Italy. Excellent versions of Verdicchio, Orvieto, and even Pinot Grigio are available for $10 or less. If you like drier versions of Chardonnay, the Vin de Pays d'Oc wines of Southern France are often good values. Some of the best examples of fruity Chardonnay you'll find for your money come from large producers in California and Australia. Look also to Australia for fruity reds such as Shiraz, which is very hard to beat for the price. As mentioned, the South of France (the Languedoc region) has a few good, inexpensive whites, but it is a gold mine for good, inexpensive reds, as is Southern Italy.

The Apulia and Abruzzi regions in Italy's southeastern corner offer a variety of dry, earthy reds for less than the price of a pizza.

Save the Rest

If you want to serve only half of a bottle each evening, buy yourself a half-bottle of a wine you like, then wash out the empty bottle with spring water and save the cork. Now, next time you open a full bottle, pour half of it into the clean half-bottle (where, tightly corked, it will keep for at least a week) and enjoy the rest of the full bottle you opened.

Stocking a Wine Cellar

Imagine being able to head to your own wine cellar for the perfect bottle of wine. For a dedicated wine lover, a well-stocked cellar has several advantages over running out to the store every time:

- The wines are purchased by the case, at a discount.
- You can always have your favorites.
- You can enjoy older vintages.
- And you can brag about having a wine cellar!

A "wine cellar" doesn't have to be a brick-lined, candlelit room full of ancient, priceless bottles. It doesn't even have to be in the cellar! A closet will do, so long as the storage area meets the following conditions:

- It's dark (constant light may be harmful over time).
- It's cool (between 50° and 65°F throughout the year).
- It's dry (excessive humidity might encourage mold).
- But it's not too dry (a little humidity prevents the corks from drying out).
- Finally, you must be able to store the wines on their sides, once again, to keep the corks moist.

Of course, you still have to come up with the wines you actually want to keep. Here are some useful guidelines for choosing wines to put in your cellar.

Wines to Keep on Hand for Special Occasions

Every now and then, a special day sneaks up on you. Whether it's an anniversary or an impromptu dinner party, here are some special wines that will fit the bill nicely:

- Californian Cabernet Sauvignon that you've aged for a couple of years.
- Carefully chosen red Burgundy or Oregon Pinot Noir.
- Less expensive Cru Classé Bordeaux or one of the better of the Cru Bourgeois Bordeaux.
- Maybe a fancy first- or second-growth Bordeaux for a very special occasion.
- Your favorite Champagne (the real thing, from France).
- A good dessert wine.

Wines Worth Aging

Not all wines benefit from a few years of aging; in fact, more and more premium producers are making "modern-style" wines that are fruitier and more enjoyable in their youth than the wines that they produced in the past. That being said, there are a great number of wines that benefit from aging in your wine cellar for a few years:

- Cabernet Sauvignon
- Châteauneuf-du-Pape
- Northern Rhônes, such as Hermitage
- Red Bordeaux
- German Rieslings
- Port and other dessert wines
- Barolo and Barbaresco from Piedmont
- Super-Tuscans, Brunello di Montalcino, Vino Nobile di Montepulciano, and riserva Chiantis from Tuscany

This list is by no means complete. Most wine reviewers give the aging potential of wines in their reviews, and a surprising number of wines—even whites—are deemed worthy of at least some short-term cellaring.

CHAPTER 9

A Consumer Revolution

The Internet has revolutionized our lives. It's changed how we communicate, shop, and consume content. And that's just a short list. Today, the Internet is also upending the wine industry. Online shopping and wine delivery services have transformed the way you can purchase wine. Wine blogs bring you breaking news in the wine industry, from top voices and critics in wine circles. And online wine clubs can show you the best wines for your palate, and bring you together with wine enthusiasts from all over the world—truly broadening your tastings and experiences. As the online wine community continues to expand, the world of wine tasting will never be the same.

Twilight of the Gatekeepers

With virtually every consumer good, from food or electronics to a simple glass of wine, consumers across the globe have grown more comfortable in looking past professional critics. Instead, many people are turning to friends and trusted networks for recommendations. You no longer have to look to the experts alone to find the best goods that suit your needs—and in the wine community, many enthusiasts are expanding their educations from the traditional print reviews or the specialists in wine country. If you're looking to learn more about wine, and acquire the wines you love the most, turn to online reviewers and writers in the blogosphere for fresh insight into the best wines in the world.

The Growth of Online Reviews

There are a plethora of examples for successful online review sites, and more than likely, you've already visited a few. Consider, for instance, the popularity of travel websites like TripAdvisor (*www.tripadvisor.com*). TripAdvisor touts itself as the "world's largest travel site," where you can browse 150 million reviews from travelers all over the world. From lush resort vacations to quiet camping trips to luxe hotels all over the world, you will find up-to-the-minute reviews of the best and worst the world has to offer—from regular folks who share your hobbies and interests. Not surprisingly, TripAdvisor has supplanted paper-based guides like Frommer's and Fodor's as a more interactive, all-inclusive, and personalized tool you can use to plan your perfect trip.

Looking for a great place to grab a bite to eat? As you may know, Yelp (*www.yelp.com*) is now the holy grail of restaurant reviews, bringing readers the best information on local eateries, both casual and upscale. You'll also find excellent reviews of the shopping, nightlife, services, and medical care in your area. Similarly, local blogs describing the best and worst of neighborhoods across the country are becoming increasingly influential when it comes to finding the best burrito or car mechanic. Even movie reviews are much different than a few years ago. It's no longer necessary to open the newspaper for reviews when you can hear from dozens of voices on websites like IMDb (*www.imdb.com*) and Rotten Tomatoes (*www.rottentomatoes.com*).

Wine Reviews Expand Online Too

In the same vein as TripAdvisor and Yelp, the online wine community has grown to share thoughts, insight, and opinions on varietals, brands, techniques, and wineries across the world. With wine, however, famous critics like Robert Parker, who popularized the 100-point scale—and publications like *Wine Spectator*, which claims nearly 3 million readers—continue to have enormous influence on the wine industry. These voices of authority have persevered, despite the growth of the online critic. But this is changing, and fast, one blog at a time.

Just look at CellarTracker (*www.cellartracker.com*). In 2003, Eric LeVine, a wine collector, built a data-management program for his wine cellar. His friends soon begged him to share it online so they could catalog their wines and record tasting notes. So LeVine made his program available to everyone, for free.

The website has become extremely popular, with nearly 1 million monthly visitors. If you are looking for in-depth analyses of different wines, this is the site to check out. In fact, each day more than 2,000 wines are reviewed on the site. This means CellarTracker users review more wines every six days than Robert Parker reviews in an entire year. And it means you have the ability to discover more wines from more critics and enthusiasts than ever before.

CellarTracker isn't just used by oenophiles. Even if you're new to the wine circles, CellarTracker, and similar sites, can introduce you to new varietals and broaden your education without requiring membership fees or an expensive trip to wine country. About nine in ten visitors are unregistered, meaning that regular wine novices and people just getting in to wine visit the site for reviews. Indeed, fewer and fewer consumers are relying on prominent critics to tell them what they should or shouldn't drink. This multiplicity of voices will change how you decide which wines to purchase, and when.

Wine Wisdom

In addition to CellarTracker, amateur critics are sharing their thoughts on personal blogs; message boards; social media platforms like Facebook, Twitter, and Instagram; and mobile apps like Delectable and Vivino.

The Golden Age of Wine Writing

Before everyone was connected to the Internet 24/7, most American wine lovers got their news and recommendations from three print sources: the *Wine Advocate*, *Wine Spectator*, and *Wine Enthusiast*. Ambitious oenophiles also read Frank Prial's weekly column in the *New York Times*, which ran from 1972 through 2004, and sought out British publications like *Decanter*.

In 2004, wine blogs started popping up. These blogs were created by wine enthusiasts who were motivated by a passion for wine as well as a desire to comment on wine-related issues the mainstream wine press either failed to cover or covered too one-dimensionally. Two of the earliest American wine blogs of note are Vinography (*www.vinography.com*), founded by Alder

Yarrow, and Fermentation (*www.fermentationwineblog.com*), founded by Tom Wark, both in 2004. Yarrow writes that in 2003, he typed "wine blog" into Google and received zero results.

Popular Wine Blog Topics Today

Aside from a poor Internet connection, there were no barriers to launching a wine blog, so the wine blogosphere quickly grew. And what started as a small collection of amateur wine journalists embracing a new form of communication has evolved into a group of writers that's virtually indistinguishable from the "conventional" wine media.

Indeed, leading wine bloggers now contribute regularly to traditional media outlets, and established print critics feel obligated to write online. Thanks to the democratization of wine writing, more people than ever before have access to more content than ever before. There are a huge number of popular topics in wine blogging today. You can find a blog about anything wine-related, from new tricks to storing wines to learning which older wines are finally being opened and enjoyed. Many people are visiting winery blogs to learn about winemaking, read about the latest harvest, and find out how older wines are drinking. As the wine business grows, more and more bloggers are writing about the intersection of politics, business, and wine. Restaurant reviews continue to remain popular in the blogosphere, giving insight to food and wine pairings across cultures and genres. Blogs can also act as platforms for wineries to promote events and give you a behind-the-scenes look at the wine industry. Regardless of what you are looking for, there is a blog out there to satisfy your interests.

Choosing a wine blog to follow depends on your personal preferences. Some blogs focus on single subjects, like red wines, while others focus on photography and video. Others may hone in on particular regions, giving you insight into the top wines in your area (or a way to decipher the label on the bottle you just purchased). Some wine blogs focus exclusively on wine tourism, giving readers a glimpse into the top wine destinations in the world, with travel tips and trip suggestions. Ultimately, the choice will come down to your interests and preferences.

Social Media and Wine

When Facebook was founded in 2004, serious wine blogs were just beginning to gain traction. Twitter arrived in 2006, when Facebook had about 12 million active users. Today, most people are constantly connected to e-mail, Facebook, Twitter, and countless other sites. The ability to connect with people across the world gives you an advantage when expanding your wine education. As you discover the voices that resonate with your wine interests and preferences, you can begin to follow those renowned critics (and humble reviewers!) on your preferred social networks. Likewise, the ability for you to connect with companies all over the world has immediate appeal, as you can discover the best deals, services, and brands for your tastes. (And wine-related companies are quickly learning that utilizing social media intelligently can help them build brands, reach consumers on a more personal level, and hopefully sell some bottles.)

Facebook

The granddaddy of all social media sites, Facebook has revolutionized the way you connect to others and share information and ideas. In wine circles, Facebook has become a great way to share the best of the wine world, where friends can exchange messages for wine suggestions, post status updates from their favorite wineries, or join wine enthusiast groups and pages where the latest industry news is announced. Liking your favorite wineries' Facebook pages will connect you instantly to their news feeds, and you'll receive updates and new posts about events, sales, new products, and more. Joining wine groups will get you in touch with other enthusiasts around the world, where you can engage in conversation about the latest hot topics, or simply enjoy how wine connects so many people together.

Twitter

Twitter is a great way for you to follow myriad experts in the wine industry. From wine critics to winemakers, oenophiles are following and connecting to each other, sharing their opinions on tastings, travel, winemaking, and other popular topics. It's also a fun medium to share your wine adventures, wherever you happen to be. Twitter users tweet their experiences from wineries and restaurants around the globe, offering insight into creative pairings, new brands, and the best varietals for the season. You can also follow wine magazines to get the latest news from the industry, keeping you informed with updates and knowledge, 24/7.

Instagram and Pinterest

Instagram, the photo and video sharing social media platform, provides users with visual inspiration when it comes to food and wine. This online service allows you to take pictures and videos of your wine experiences, tastings, and travel, and share them on a variety of social networking services, from Facebook to Tumblr to Twitter. By following your friends, fellow wine lovers, and wine experts, you'll discover gorgeous photography and video that details the world of wine from incredible perspectives. And by sharing your own photos and videos, you'll acquire followers that share your interest in and passion for wine.

Likewise, Pinterest allows you to share your interests visually, by posting photos or videos to online "pinboards," and browsing what other viewers have shared. In the wine community, Pinterest has inspired thousands of boards for wine travel, wine humor, wine restaurants, party ideas, shopping lists, vineyards, accessories, and more.

Wine Apps

Mobile apps are a great way for you to detail and record your wine experiences on the go. There are apps that will track the bottles and varietals you've tried, with rating options, pricing information, and availability information by region. Apps are also a fun way for you to learn more about wine in general, with information and definitions on particular varietals, brands, and pricing. Some apps offer suggestions on how to choose wines by style, region, or grape, and how to pick the best wine to match the food you serve. Wine enthusiasts now have a wealth of knowledge at their fingertips, and the apps you choose can expand your knowledge exponentially.

Connect to Wineries Through VinTank

VinTank, a social intelligence firm out of Napa Valley, is helping wineries everywhere adapt to this rapidly changing technological world. The company's founder, Paul Mabray, speaks regularly about the impact of social media on the wine world. As he once explained on the VinTank website, "Whereas in the past producers pretty much entrusted retailers with the task of managing consumer relationships on an ongoing basis, they can now connect directly with friends, fans, and followers. [By embracing social media,] they can gain insight into who their fans are, what interests them, what they're talking about, whether or not they have plans to travel to wine country, and a whole lot more—regardless of what channel they purchased the wine in. That's pretty powerful stuff."

Linking Wine Consumers and Sellers

It's important for everyone in the wine industry, from wineries, to seasoned wine tasters, to amateur oenophiles, to stay connected with one another, because this is how people learn. Take for example Cornerstone Cellars, a small winery out of Napa Valley with a tasting room in the heart of Yountville. Cornerstone produces about 10,000 cases of wine each year and employs just seven people. The CEO, Craig Camp, has urged his entire team to engage with consumers on social media. The company has been tremendously successful as a result.

Suppose, for example, you are a steakhouse patron in Kansas City, and you praise a wine from Cornerstone on Twitter or Instagram. There's a good chance that Cornerstone's CEO will thank you, and then extend an invitation to visit Cornerstone's tasting room. This personalized touch results in visits virtually every day. It's that easy for you to make a connection with professionals in the wine business.

Making connections on social media is as beneficial for you, the wine consumer, as it is for the seller. Following certain wineries and wine sellers on social media is the perfect way to stay on top of new wine releases and industry news. This is, without question, the future of the wine industry: keeping everyone connected. Staying active on your favorite social media platforms will keep you in the loop, too.

Envisioning Wine's Future

If you need evidence of the future of wine, look no further than your closest grocery store. Thirty years ago, the local market sold little more than jug wine like Gallo's Hearty Burgundy—if wine was even stocked. Today, the average upscale supermarket carries 1,500 wine selections or more. The number of breakfast cereals pales in comparison. As the number of choices has increased, consumers have shown that they are eager to learn.

From Supermarkets to Specialty Stores

Consider the rise of specialty wine shops. Around the United States you'll find boutique retailers who are filling their shelves with interesting, small-production wines— and helping consumers learn about wine by paying attention to their preferences, offering food-and-wine pairing advice, and answering questions without judgment. Or look at wine bars. They're sprouting up from coast to coast, providing opportunities for people to explore wines. Take for example Trader Joe's. When you visit this store, along with picking up your fruits and veggies, you can grab a bottle of Charles Shaw's Two Buck Chuck.

Changing Tide

Today's wine drinkers are eager to visit these retailers and wine bars and sample obscure varieties from obscure regions. Trousseau from France's Jura, perhaps? Or maybe some Ribolla Gialla from northeast Italy? The diversity of what's available is greater than ever before—and more and more consumers are drinking adventurously.

High-end restaurants are also approaching wine differently. Whereas sommeliers were once glorified sales agents who intimidated guests by pushing expensive, predictable wines, today's sommeliers are wine educators, eager to share their passion and palates. Most are keen to help you, the patron, find the perfect wine, regardless of budget.

This list could go on. Bookstores are now packed with easy-to-navigate wine guides. Wine classes are more popular than ever before. All these efforts help demystify wine. The world of wine is clearly changing, and you are the key. In the optimistic future of American wine, well-informed consumers will be confident in their own preferences and eager to explore without consulting a "professional." So grab a glass and enjoy!

APPENDIX

Glossary

acidity
Naturally occurring acids in grapes that are vital components for the life, vitality, and balance of all wines.

aging
Maturing process of a wine to improve its taste.

alcohol
The major component in wine. Also known as ethyl alcohol.

appellation
The official geographical location where the grapes used in the wine are grown.

aroma
The smell of a wine.

astringent
The puckering sensation in the mouth attributable to the tannins and acids found in some wines.

austere
A tasting term that is used to describe young wines that have not yet developed a discernable aroma.

balance
A tasting term that describes how well a wine's components complement each other.

barrel
A container used to store or ferment wine.

big
This term is used to describe wines that are of full of flavor and with high levels of tannins, alcohol, and grape flavor extracts.

bite
A result of good levels of acidity (especially in young wines).

bitter
Unpleasant taste that registers at the back of the tongue.

blanc de blancs
A white wine—most often sparkling—made exclusively from white grapes.

blanc de noirs
A white or slightly tinted wine—and usually sparkling—made exclusively from red grapes.

blend
The technique of mixing wines of different varieties, regions, and barrels from different years.

body
Perception of fullness or texture in the mouth due primarily to the wine's alcohol.

bottle aging
Allowing wine to acquire complexity, depth, and texture in the bottle.

bouquet
The combination of flowery and fruity aromas that come from the alcohols and acids in a wine.

breathe
Allowing air to mix with a wine to develop its flavor.

brut
Dry style of Champagne and sparkling wine.

capsule
The protective cover of tin, lead, aluminum, or plastic that is placed over the top of a bottle of wine to insulate the wine from outside influences.

Cava
The Spanish term for sparkling wines made using the traditional Champagne method.

character
A wine's features and style.

clarity
The appearance of wine that has no cloudiness.

clean
Wines that are straightforward and have no unpleasant odors or flavors.

cloudy
The opposite of clarity; wine that is visually unclear.

complex
Nuances of flavors of a wine often achieved with aging.

cork
The spongy material from the bark of the cork tree used to seal wine bottles.

corked
Wines that have the smell of wood dry rot resulting from a defective cork.

crisp
Wines with good acidity and taste without excessive sweetness.

cru
French term meaning "growth."

cuvée
Blend; in the production of Champagne, cuvée is the specific blend of still wines used as a base for Champagne.

decanting
Pouring wine from a bottle into a carafe or decanter.

depth
Wines with full-bodied, intense, and complex flavors.

disgorging
Removing sediment from a bottle of Champagne following secondary fermentation.

dry
Opposite of sweet. All the sugar from the grapes has been converted to alcohol during fermentation.

earthy
Flavors derived from the soil where the grapes have been grown.

enology
The study of wine and winemaking; also oenology.

extra dry
Champagne classification where there is a slight perception of sweetness.

fat
A big, soft, and silky wine that fills the mouth.

fermentation
The process that turns grape juice into wine. The enzymes in the yeast convert sugar into alcohol and carbon dioxide.

fining
Clarifying young wine before bottling to remove impurities.

finish
The aftertaste or impression a wine leaves after it's swallowed.

fortified wine
Wine whose alcohol content is increased by adding brandy or neutral spirits.

fruity
The flavor or aroma of fruits in wine.

hard
An abundance of tannin or acidity.

ice wine
Extremely sweet wines made from grapes that have been frozen on the vines prior to harvest; also called Eiswein.

late-harvest wine
Wine made from ripe grapes left on the vine for periods in excess of their normal picking times,

resulting in an extreme concentration of sugar.

lees
The sediment of yeasts and small grape particles that settle in the barrel as wine develops.

maceration
Technique of fermenting uncrushed grapes under pressure to produce fresh, fruity wine.

magnum
A bottle holding 1.5 liters, or the equivalent of two standard bottles.

Meritage
Term used for both red and white American wines that are produced by blending traditional Bordeaux grape varietals.

nutty
A fine, crisp flavor often found in sherries and fine white wines.

oak
The flavor imparted to wine by barrel aging. It can be best described as a toasty or woodlike flavor. Sometimes a vanilla flavor will be imparted by fine oak to the wine.

oxidation
Exposure of wine to air, which causes chemical changes and deterioration.

pigeage
A French term for the traditional stomping of grapes by foot.

press
The piece of equipment used to gently separate grape juice from grape skins.

punt
The indentation at the base of a wine or Champagne bottle, which reinforces the bottle's structure.

reserve
A term without a legal definition in the United States but often used to designate a special wine.

richness
Rich wines have well-balanced flavors and intrinsic power.

sec
A term that, when applied to Champagne, describes a relatively sweet wine. Used in the context of still wines, the term means dry—without any residual sugar.

secondary fermentation
The process of converting still wine into Champagne that takes place in the bottle. In the production of still wines, the term is sometimes used in place of malolactic fermentation.

sommelier
French term for "wine waiter."

The Book of Wine

spumante
The Italian term for fully sparkling wines as opposed to those that are slightly sparkling—frizzante.

tannin
Substance found naturally in wine from the skin, pulp, and stalks. Tannins are responsible for the astringent quality found in wine, especially red wines. Tannins form the basis for the long life of wines, and while they can be overpowering in young wines, with bottle aging they tend to become softer.

terroir
Literally "the soil." A French term referring to the particular character (aromas and flavors) of a given vineyard—or even a small part of that vineyard.

thin
Wines that lack fullness, depth, and complexity.

varietal
A wine named after the grape from which it is produced. In California, for instance, a wine labeled "Pinot Noir" must by law consist of at least 75 percent Pinot Noir grapes.

vineyard
The place where grapes are grown.

vinification
The process of making wine.

vintage
Harvest year of grapes and the resulting wines made from them. Ninety-five percent of the wine in a vintage-designated bottle must be from grapes harvested in that year.

viticulture
The practice (art, science, and philosophy) of growing grapevines.

woody
In most wines this is an undesirable condition indicating that there is a taint of some type from defective wood or an overuse of new oak.

yeast
Naturally occurring, single-celled organisms found on the skins of grapes that are the primary promoters of fermentation. In the fermentation process, yeast turns sugar into alcohol and carbon dioxide.

INDEX

The Book of Wine